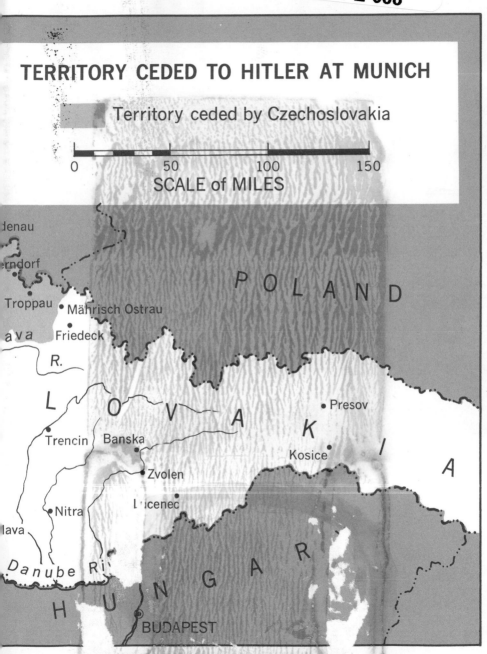

TERRITORY CEDED TO HITLER AT MUNICH

Territory ceded by Czechoslovakia

0   50   100   150
SCALE of MILES

denau

rndorf

Troppau • Mährisch Ostrau

ava   • Friedeck

R.

POLAND

L   O   V   A   K   I

• Presov

• Trencin   Banska •

Kosice •

A

• Zvolen

L icenec

• Nitra

lava

Danube R.

H   U   N   G   A   R

• BUDAPEST

BETRAYAL

THE MUNICH PACT OF 1938

BETRAYAL

THE MUNICH PACT OF 1938

BY IRVING WERSTEIN

DOUBLEDAY & COMPANY, INC.

GARDEN CITY, NEW YORK

940.53 0199205
Wer

To Goldie with love.

AUTHOR'S NOTE

Seldom has there been a year more memorable historically than 1938. A civil war raged in Spain between forces of the legal Spanish Republic and Fascists led by a clique of generals under Francisco Franco.

In a sense, the Spanish Civil War was really an international conflict; both sides received outside help. Soviet Russia provided the Republicans or Loyalists with guns, tanks, planes, and technicians. Foreign volunteers from many lands, including the United States, formed international brigades which fought valiantly on behalf of the Madrid government.

The Nationalists (rebels) were bolstered by Fascist Italy and Nazi Germany. Benito Mussolini, the Duce (leader) of Italy, sent not only planes, tanks, and munitions, but also more than fifty thousand soldiers—four fully equipped divisions—to fight for Franco. His contributions, although not matched in quantity, were surpassed in quality by Nazi Germany.

Adolf Hitler's Luftwaffe (Air Force) pilots gained combat experience in Spain; their warplanes, such as Heinkels, Fokkers, and Dorniers, were tested in battle against Soviet-made fighters.

The Spanish Civil War has been justly called a rehearsal for World War II.

In 1938, the United States, still grappling with the effects of the Depression, was more concerned with its internal problems than with external ones. A spirit of isolationism pervaded the nation and influenced many of its leaders; but Americans soon learned that neither the Atlantic nor the Pacific Oceans were sufficient barriers to insulate them from the world's troubles.

7

The word "appeasement" gained new meaning when the Munich Pact was signed in September 1938. Less than a year after the agreement, which had been heralded as assurance of "peace for our time," the Second World War broke out.

I have attempted here to present a picture of those days when shortsighted men gave in to the threat of force. For many young readers, 1938 may seem as distant as the Ice Age, but the impact of what happened three decades ago is still felt today. (In 1968, Czechoslovakia again became the scene of a dramatic confrontation between democracy and autocracy, when Soviet troops, aided by Poles, Hungarians, and East Germans occupied that unhappy country.)

The principals in the strange drama of Munich have vanished into history, but what they did continues to pose burning questions. At what point must free men stand fast and fight to retain their freedom? Where is the line beyond which "negotiation" becomes "appeasement," and when does "appeasement" become "surrender"?

The answers are not to be found in this book; only future history will provide them. Obviously, in a work of this scope, I could not present a definitive study of the Munich Pact and its background. It is a tale of intrigue and political chicanery too complex for a book such as this. In attempting to illuminate the event and the times I compressed some details and glossed over others. However, this is essentially the story of the Munich Pact.

I wish to stress that any dialogue attributed to historical personages is taken from eyewitness accounts, stenographic reports, and other authenticated sources. I have taken no liberties with history by putting words into people's mouths.

In researching this work, I consulted books, documents, newspapers, magazines, and manuscripts. For the general reader I recommend several interesting and informative books: William Shirer's *The Rise and Fall of the Third Reich* is an excellent study of the Hitler years. Mr. Shirer also is unsurpassed for background material. *Munich* by Keith Eubank is a superb presentation of the pact and how it came about; on a par with Eubank's work is *Munich: Peace For Our Time* by Henri Nogueres. This book also contains some incisive and revealing profiles of the men of Munich.

Other compelling books on the subject are: *The Life of Neville*

Chamberlain by Keith Feiling; *Munich: Prologue to Tragedy* by John W. Wheeler-Bennett, and Telford Taylor's *Sword and Swastika*.

I take this opportunity for thanking all who helped me in completing *Betrayal: The Munich Pact of 1938*. Sid Solomon and Henry Chafetz of Pageant Book Company tracked down long-out-of-print source materials. The staffs of the New York Public Library and the New-York Historical Society Library gave willing and cheerful assistance. I owe a special acknowledgment to my editor, Mr. John Ernst, not only for his patience at missed deadlines, but also for valuable suggestions and skillful editing. My agent, Miss Candida Donadio, was always there with both persuasion and encouragement when this author floundered. Mrs. Lee Levin deserves a salute for efficiently typing an often nearly illegible manuscript.

New York, May 1968.   I.W.

BETRAYAL

THE MUNICH PACT OF 1938

"When I come back I hope I may be able to say, as Hotspur says in Shakespeare's *Henry IV,* 'Out of this nettle, danger, we pluck this flower, safety.'"

> Neville Chamberlain, on the morning of his departure for Munich, September 29, 1938.

"They that can give up essential liberty to obtain a little temporary safety deserve neither liberty nor safety. . . ."

> Benjamin Franklin

CHAPTER 1

In the fall of 1918, the German Imperial Army was barely able to continue fighting. Its divisions were shattered, its manpower dwindling. Once-proud regiments that had marched to the gates of Paris were reduced to tattered remnants. The Germans were pounded and battered by powerful Allied armies.

The British and French, almost on the verge of defeat for three years, had been bolstered by the American Expeditionary Force —two million fresh, young soldiers who brought new enthusiasm and vigor to the Allied cause.

By September 28, 1918, General Erich Ludendorff, of the German High Command, urged the government to seek an armistice "at once." He was backed in this demand by the Commander-in-Chief of the German Imperial Army, Field Marshal Paul von Hindenburg.

In Berlin, four days later, the field marshal personally told a meeting of the Crown Council, presided over by Kaiser Wilhelm II, "The Army can wait no longer, not even two days, for an armistice. . . . We have played this game to the end. . . . The military situation is very bad for us. . . . It is imperative that we stop the fighting now. . . ."

Despite the recommendations of Hindenburg, Ludendorff, and others, however, the war dragged on for another month. During this period, the Imperial Army's position grew even more desperate.

Ironically, the collapse that brought on the armistice did not take place on the battlefield; it happened in Berlin on November

9, 1918, when Kaiser Wilhelm abdicated his throne and fled to exile in Holland.

That same day, with the dynasty dissolved, the militaristic autocracy swept away, a German Republic was proclaimed. On November 11, 1918, civilian members of that rump government signed the armistice with the Allies and the guns fell silent along the battlefronts. For the first time since August 1914, Europe was at peace.

The creation of the German Republic was greeted with enthusiasm in the Allied nations. At last, statesmen declared, Germany would have democratic government; no longer would the Fatherland menace neighboring countries.

Germany, some predicted, was about to enter an era of "peace and democracy." After all, had not the Kaiser's troops been thoroughly beaten? Rarely in history had any nation and her allies suffered such an overwhelming military disaster as befell the Central Powers—Germany, the Austro-Hungarian Empire, Bulgaria, and Turkey. Was it not reasonable to suppose that these nations would avoid war in the future?

The heads of the German Army were expert professional soldiers. They had recognized and accepted the dreary fact that the war was lost. They had been the first to demand an armistice. But even in defeat, they sought to salvage the Army's prestige.

No doubt, the Allies would have been less optimistic about the German Republic had they realized that the General Staff never intended to relinquish any of the influence they had held in Germany for many years. Under Kaiser or Republic, they were determined to retain their position.

Forces were at work in Germany which almost guaranteed the Army's dominance. Only a year earlier, in November 1917, the Bolsheviks led by Nicolai Lenin had seized power in Russia. The specter of communism now haunted Germany. In Berlin, the Communist leaders, Karl Liebknecht and Rosa Luxemburg, were rallying numerous followers to take over the country. The possibility of a Soviet Germany seemed a frighteningly real one.

The reins of government were reluctantly held by the German Social Democratic Party. Their chief, Friedrich Ebert, a saddlemaker, was terrified at the prospect of social revolution.

Berlin was in a state of chaos on November 9, 1918: A general strike paralyzed the capital; there was rioting in the streets. Worst of all, the Communists were fomenting insurrection. Liebknecht and Luxemburg, who had set up headquarters in the Kaiser's palace, were preparing to announce the formation of Soldiers' and Workers' Councils (Soviets) not only in Berlin, but throughout Germany.

The frantic Social Democrats held an emergency meeting, and a huge crowd gathered outside the Reichstag, where the Socialists were conferring.

If it had been left up to Ebert, Germany would have kept the monarchy in a constitutional form, similar to that of England. The ex-saddlemaker favored offering the crown to some blood relative of the Kaiser; it made little difference which one, just so long as he was of royal Hohenzollern descent. But the noisy crowd in the street were fed up with kaisers, kings, and hereditary rulers. They called for freedom, democracy, liberty.

The cries "All power to the Soviets!" and "Long live Bolshevism!" were raised by thousands. These slogans resounded in the Socialist Party's chambers, thoroughly frightening the assembled deputies.

Philip Scheidemann, co-leader of the Socialists, yanked open the French doors that led to the balcony and stepped out, raising his hands for silence. The restive crowd grew quiet. In that second, Scheidemann profoundly influenced German history.

He announced the formation of a republic, with Ebert as President of the provisional government. The President-designate was shocked and angry. This was not what he had wanted. There was no chance now for a constitutional monarchy and the restoration of the Hohenzollern dynasty. The wild acclaim accorded Scheidemann's unexpected announcement gave clear evidence of this.

So Friedrich Ebert became the first President of the German Republic, a government destined to last only fifteen years. The reasons for its short existence were many, the main one being that from the outset no real foundation was laid for a democratic regime.

The Republic might have thrived had the Socialists firmly believed in it. But Ebert and his colleagues were barely lukewarm to the idea. If they gave the Republic only halfhearted support, there was not likely to be any backing for it from conservative Germans.

The groups which neither could nor would support a democratic regime were the Junker landlords of East Prussia; the aristocrats; the industrialists; the Officers Corps; and the General Staff, which controlled the Army. Were a democratic Republic to endure in Germany, such bulwarks of the establishment would have had to be checked and a complete revamping of Germany's social, political, and economic structure undertaken.

Ebert was not the man to perform the necessary drastic surgery; he and Scheidemann stood for gradual change. Through the years, the Social Democrats had gained many concessions for German workers. These had been obtained not by revolutionary means but through trade union action. Most of the Socialist leaders were in fact veterans of the trade union movement, well-meaning reformers, unlike the Communists, who intended to overthrow the system rather than refine it.

Because they accepted the traditional order of German society, the founders of the Republic turned to the Army, the most authoritarian force in the country, to block the impending Communist insurrection.

On the very night the Republic was born, Ebert made a deal with the military. He told a high-ranking officer, General Wilhelm Groener, that if the Army helped put down the Communists (known in Germany as Spartacists), the Republic would maintain the Army in all its past influence and traditions and Field Marshal von Hindenburg would be retained as commander-in-chief.

That promise doomed the Republic along with the Socialists and every other liberal or progressive element in Germany. The Republic became the Army's whipping boy.

In response to Allied demands, the Germans sent a delegation to Compiègne Forest near Paris. Metting in a railroad car on November 11, 1918 with Allied military plenipotentiaries, the Germans signed the armistice agreement. Significantly, not one important officer accompanied the German armistice truce team.

The men who signed the armistice were Socialist civilians, of whom several were Jews. This was the basis for the myth German militarists later spread that the Army had not lost the war, but had been "stabbed in the back" by the "November traitors" and the Jews.

CHAPTER 2

After the armistice was signed, conditions inside Germany grew more turbulent than ever. The Spartacists continued to agitate for a Soviet Germany. Led by Liebknecht and Luxemburg—both of whom happened to be Jewish—Soldiers' and Workers' Councils were formed throughout Germany.

The soviets assumed control in many localities and the possibility of a Communist takeover increased. Middle- and upper-class Germans were fearful that the country was following the path of Russia. Newspapers labeled Ebert "The German Kerensky."

In mid-December the First Soviet Congress of Germany convened in Berlin with several hundred delegates from Soldiers' and Workers' Councils, representing every section of the country. The Congress put forward radical demands, which included the dismissal of Von Hindenburg, the abolition of the Regular Army, and the formation of a civil guard, responsible to the Soldiers' and Workers' Councils, with officers elected by the men.

This was too much for the military caste. Von Hindenburg defied the Congress by refusing to resign. President Ebert ignored the demands, but the Army pressed him to take strong measures against the Spartacists. While Ebert equivocated, the Communists acted. On December 23, 1918, a force of sailors known as the People's Marine Division, which was under Spartacist control, attacked the Chancellery and other government buildings in what appeared to be an attempt to overthrow the government. Ebert called upon the Army for aid and General Groener rushed a Regular regiment to Berlin. Before the troops arrived, the rebellious

19

sailors retired to the Imperial Palace and barricaded themselves in the royal stables.

Groener's troops attacked the Red sailors on Christmas Eve, and Berlin's holiday festivities, already subdued, were further marred by civil strife. Von Hindenburg and Groener pressed Ebert to "eliminate the Bolshevist menace." If the Republic did not act, the generals intended taking matters into their own hands.

Rather than risk facing an Army coup, Ebert declared civil war on the Spartacists and appointed Gustav Noske as Minister of National Defense. Noske, a veteran Social Democrat, was the party's "strong-arm" man. A master butcher in his youth, he had a physique that suited the trade. Noske was absolutely fearless, and gave short shrift to any person or group that endangered the Socialist Party.

When ordered to "suppress" the Spartacists, Noske went to work energetically. From January 10 to 19 he attacked with Regular Army troops and so-called Frei Korps (Free Corps) volunteers. The Spartacists resisted valiantly, but futilely. After seven days of combat the Spartacist threat was eliminated. Rosa Luxemburg and Karl Liebknecht were kidnaped and executed by Army officers.

Once the Spartacist uprisings had been broken and the Soldiers' and Workers' Councils dissolved, Ebert called for the election of a National Assembly. He felt it was time that Germany had a stable and established government.

Although the Socialists won more seats in the Assembly than any other party, they did not have a majority, and a coalition cabinet was formed. While all the parties in the government supported the Republic, each also sought to reinstate the Kaiser.

The National Assembly's first task was to draw up a constitution. For this purpose it met in Weimar on February 6, 1919. The constitution which the Assembly produced after six months of debate was an extraordinary document. On paper at least, no people were freer or more democratically governed than the Germans under the Weimar Constitution. As a blueprint for democracy it was perfect; but so many safeguards had been introduced to protect all the freedoms it guaranteed that one canceled out the other. The Weimar Constitution was to prove unworkable.

Despite its inherent defects, the Weimar Constitution was hailed by both the Germans and their former enemies. Passed overwhelm-

20

ingly in the National Assembly on July 31, 1919, it was signed by President Ebert on August 31.

During the period the Weimar Constitution was being drawn up, another document, also affecting Germany's future, was in the process of preparation at Versailles, France. This was the peace treaty —officially, the Treaty of Versailles—which detailed the balance sheet that Germany would have to pay for the war.

Cloaked in unfounded optimism, the Germans chose to believe that the Allies would be generous. Many Germans felt that their former enemies should be grateful to them. Had not Germany purged her Communists, forced out the Kaiser, and established a democratic republic? What more could the Allies ask?

"Why should the victors be vindictive? Victors can afford to show magnanimity," a Berlin newspaper editorialized.

The terms of the treaty published on May 7, 1919, after having been drafted without consulting the Germans, evoked a furious reaction. Large meetings were held objecting to the treaty, which was called "unrealizable and unbearable" by President Ebert.

The Versailles Treaty called for the ceding of some German-held territory. Alsace-Lorraine, taken in the Franco-Prussian War, was returned to France. A piece of Schleswig, wrested from Denmark in another war, was also to be given back—but only after a plebiscite. Some regions in East Prussia were awarded to Poland, which now had a corridor to the sea at Danzig. This zone separated East Prussia from the Fatherland and infuriated the Germans, many of whom considered the Poles an inferior race.

Just as infuriating was a clause which forced Germany to admit full responsibility for starting the war and a demand that Kaiser Wilhelm II and several hundred other "war criminals" be turned over to the Allies for trial.

A huge reparations charge was placed upon Germany; the full amount would be decided at a later date, but in the first two years—1919–21—five billion dollars in gold marks were to be paid the Allies, plus other sums in cattle, lumber, coal, iron, shipping, and machinery.

But the most irksome clause, from the German viewpoint, was that which limited the nation's military and naval power. The Army was restricted to one hundred thousand long-term volunteers, and was permitted neither planes nor armor. The General Staff was

21

outlawed, and the Navy reduced to little more than a token force. Submarines were forbidden, as were warships of more than ten thousand tons.

The Versailles Treaty did not destroy the country geographically, and to a large extent left her economically and politically intact. By no stretch of the imagination could it be considered a slap on the wrist. But neither was it a "degradation and humiliation," as the German press branded it. Germany had lost the war, and this was the price of defeat.

"Does one dare dwell upon the terms of a peace treaty drawn up by a victorious Germany?" a British negotiator asked.

At first, Berlin wanted to reject the terms, disavow the armistice, and continue the war. Field Marshal von Hindenburg declared, ". . . there is doubt that such an operation could succeed . . . but as a soldier, I cannot help feeling that it were better to perish honorably than accept a disgraceful peace. . . ." This high-flown sentiment was for public consumption. Privately the revered field marshal told Groener, "You know as well as I do that armed resistance is impossible for us. . . ."

The Allies, meanwhile, were growing impatient over German delay. An ultimatum was sent to Berlin. Either the treaty terms were accepted by 2:00 P.M. June 24, or else the Allies would void the armistice and "take whatever steps might be considered necessary. . . ."

In the face of this undisguised threat, Ebert appealed to the Army leaders for guidance. He would abide by their advice. Was it to be a dictated and onerous peace or a war to preserve German "honor"?

Since Von Hindenburg and Groener had already agreed that resistance would be suicidal, the word had to be given to Ebert and the people of Germany. Logically, Von Hindenburg, as the nation's most respected soldier, should have delivered the Army's verdict, but the field marshal was too conscious of his reputation to take such action. In the eyes of most Germans, he was still a hero; he wanted his image to remain unchanged. And so it was General Groener who brought the Army's decision to Ebert; it was Groener who had to bear the public's resentment.

Ebert and the National Assembly were relieved that the Army had assumed responsibility for accepting the Versailles Treaty.

22

The deputies voted overwhelmingly in favor of signing. The decision was communicated to the Allies only a few minutes before the deadline. On June 28, in the Hall of Mirrors at Versailles, the German delegation signed the treaty. From that moment, hatred of the treaty became a part of German life. The feeling against the treaty reached into every segment of German society; workers, peasants, students, businessmen, housewives were united in their rancor and resentment. To these people, the Versailles Treaty was a symbol of national humiliation and degradation.

It did not take long for the public to forget that the Army had made the decision to accept the terms of the treaty. Ultimately blame fell on the Socialists, the Communists, the Jews, who were made the scapegoats for Germany's decline.

Many voices expressed these feelings in Germany, but none more passionately than that of an odd, mustached man who wore ill-fitting clothes and harangued small crowds on street corners and in shabby halls. Born in Austria of a family named Schickelgruber Adolf Hitler, as he became known, had been in turn an artist, house painter, paperhanger, vagabond, and political adventurer. Like so many of his contemporaries, Hitler had fought in the 1914–18 war. His military career was neither distinguished nor meteoric; the highest rank he attained was Feldwebel, or corporal.

But this obscure Feldwebel had grand dreams for himself and for Germany, the adopted land he loved with maniacal passion. When the Fatherland was defeated and forced to accept the Versailles Treaty, Hitler swore to devote his life to a German resurgence.

He joined a splinter political party, which eventually became the National Socialist German Workers Party, known by the acronym Nazi. The Nazi Party was a perfect springboard for Hitler, who proved to be a brilliant rabblerouser, capable of inspiring an audience to hysterical enthusiasm.

In the beginning, Hitler spoke only to handfuls of people at a time, but gradually his audiences grew until they numbered in thousands. Word spread throughout Bavaria, where his efforts were centered, that the ex-corporal had some ideas worthy of attention. Hitler harped mainly on the inequities of the Versailles

23

Treaty, the ineptness of the Weimar Republic, and the baseness of the "November traitors," the Jews, and the radicals.

"Germany must be cleansed! Germany must be purified! Germany must rise again to her rightful place in the world!" Hitler declared. "But that can be achieved only when the Fatherland is purged of the mongrel scum that led our beloved nation into the depths! The Jews! The Bolsheviks! The fainthearted cowards of November 1918!"

CHAPTER 3

The Weimar Republic, led by lukewarm Socialists, lacked the vigor to fight extremists from the right or the left. Ebert detested violence; when conservatives began undermining the Republic, he did little to suppress them. Though he hated the Communists, Ebert seldom used force when they acted against the Republic. He catered to the Army, returning the one-hundred-thousand-man Reichswehr (Army) to the same authoritarian officers who had led Germany during the War. By clinging to the old, autocratic ways, the Socialists permitted the Army to be the nation's master, rather than its servant.

Hitler shrewdly played upon German militaristic pride; again and again he stressed that only when the Army threw off the yoke of Versailles and Germany was ruled by "pure-blooded" Germans or Aryans, instead of Jews and traitors, would the nation once more be a world power.

Increasing numbers of Bavarians began to listen seriously to Hitler during the early 1920s when the country's economic conditions worsened. A devastating business slump hit Germany in 1921. The mark dropped to an exchange rate of seven thousand to the dollar at the beginning of 1923. Factories closed, unemployment soared. Because Germany could not meet her reparations payments to France, the French occupied the Ruhr, the heart of Germany's industrial production, and threatened to stay there until the reparations bill was paid.

By the end of January 1923, the mark's value stood at eighteen thousand to the dollar. But even this was not the bottom; by the year's end it took four billion marks to buy a dollar. The German economy was a shambles. Workers, the middle class, and even the very wealthy were financially ruined. Nothing like this had ever happened under the Kaiser. It was easy enough to blame the Jew-inspired, Socialist-run democratic republic for bringing the Fatherland to disaster.

Hitler spoke nightly, rousing the people, building a following. By November 9, 1923, he believed he had enough strength to take power in Bavaria.

Mobilizing a force of Storm Troopers—uniformed toughs who guarded Nazi Party meetings—Hitler organized and led what has become known as "the Munich Beer Hall Putsch." (In German a *putsch* is the forcible seizure of power.)

Hitler's revolt turned into a tragicomedy which cost the lives of nineteen men—sixteen Nazis and three police officers. Participating in the abortive uprising were such future Nazi leaders as Hermann Goering, Ernst Roehm, and Julius Streicher.

Also marching with Hitler was General Erich Ludendorff, who had become a follower of the Nazis. Ludendorff escaped unscathed from the shooting, but broke with Hitler after the failure of the *putsch*. From that day in November 1923 until he died fourteen years later, Ludendorff never again spoke to Hitler.

As a result of the Beer Hall Putsch, Hitler was sentenced to a four-year prison term during which he wrote *Mein Kampf* (My Struggle), a ponderous book which detailed his philosophy and was to become the Nazi bible.

When Hitler left Landsberg Prison in 1927, much had changed in Germany. The Socialists no longer controlled the government; Ebert had died in 1925 and was succeeded by Field Marshal Paul von Hindenburg, the candidate of the conservative industrialists and businessmen.

The German mark had been stabilized; business was good. Most Germans were working, making money, living well. In such prosperous times, the Versailles Treaty, the "November traitors," and anti-Semitism ceased to be major issues.

The Nazis had lost most of their following, and Hitler found the party at a low ebb. But the situation changed after the international stock market crash of 1929, which brought on a worldwide economic depression. Once more there was chaos and despair in Germany. Soon Germans began returning to the Nazi Party.

26

The people, confused and frightened, received little reassurance from the Weimar Republic. Indeed, the government added to the turmoil. From 1929–33, a half dozen or more Cabinets fell. New faces, new coalitions, new stopgap measures failed to forestall crises that followed in staggering succession: financial troubles, labor strife, unemployment, social unrest. The Republic was threatened by Communists on the left and Nazis on the right. Seldom before had any nation been as bedeviled as was Germany during those four years.

Hitler flourished in the atmosphere of doom that pervaded the land. His flaming speeches aroused the masses. Hailed by the Nazis as Fuehrer (leader), Hitler gave the embittered German people a scapegoat for all their woes: the Jews. The Jews, he claimed, had lost the war; the Jews had signed the armistice; the Jews had accepted the Versailles Treaty. Purge them from Germany and the nation would be saved. Along with the Jews Hitler wanted to drive out the Communists, Socialists, trade unionists, intellectuals, visionaries, and "degenerates." He called for the establishment of a new Germany based on the idea of the supremacy of the Aryan race.

The Fuehrer spoke of a New Order, a Third Reich, which would become the greatest power on earth. The First Reich had been the medieval Holy Roman Empire. The Second Reich was created by Bismarck in 1870. Both had brought glory to Germany. Hitler promised a Germany of unlimited scope, a Germany unmatched in all history. "Today, Germany! Tomorrow, the world!" he cried.

Incredibly, Adolf Hitler, out of favor in 1927, became Chancellor of Germany, appointed by Von Hindenburg on January 30, 1933, after striking Nazi election victories.

Once in office, Hitler plotted the destruction of the Weimar Republic. Hindenburg died August 2, 1934, and his death cleared from Hitler's path the last obstacle to dictatorship in Germany. The Nazi chieftain declared himself Fuehrer of Germany. He was now the nation's absolute ruler, master of eighty-four million Germans. Many Germans responded wholeheartedly to the Fuehrer. In their eyes he was a messiah come to carry them from the depths of defeat and depression to new heights of triumph.

By 1938, it was obvious that Hitler was leading his fanatical followers to war. He flouted the Versailles Treaty, rebuilt the Ger-

27

man Army, created a mighty Air Force and a small but powerful Navy. In defiance of Great Britain and France, he boldly reoccupied the industrial Ruhr Basin, the Rhineland and the Saar, all stripped from Germany by the terms of the Versailles Treaty.

France and Great Britain objected to these moves, but did not try to stop them. The Allies shrank from military action. In the words of one British politician: "This was no cause for war. The Germans merely were re-entering their own back yard. . . ."

The Fuehrer carried out his threat to make Germany Judenrein —purged of Jews. Those hapless people were terrorized, pauperized, beaten, murdered. Thousands of them fled from Germany. Millions more remained and eventually died in concentration camps.

The fifth anniversary of the Hitler regime was celebrated in February 1938. The Fuehrer's achievements in that brief period were remarkable: enforced labor had eliminated unemployment; German industry, geared to build tanks, planes, guns, and ships, was booming; the Wehrmacht (Army) boasted sixty or seventy splendidly equipped divisions; no nation in Europe equaled Germany in tanks; the Luftwaffe numbered five thousand bomber and fighter planes, the world's strongest air force.

If the German Navy was small, it had many submarines and several "pocket battleships" such as the *Scharnhorst* and the *Gneisneau,* and the forty-five-thousand-ton battleship *Bismarck*.

Hitler knew his potential enemies were woefully weak. The British Army consisted of only a few divisions. Great Britain's Navy was still stronger than his own, but the odds had been whittled down. The Royal Air Force (RAF) was appreciably smaller than the Luftwaffe, and its planes were no match for Germany's. The new-model British aircraft—Hurricanes and Spitfires—had barely gone into production.

France, which had suffered terribly in the 1914–18 war, could mobilize a one-hundred-division Army, but the French General Staff had abandoned its traditional policy of spirited attack. Appalled by her tremendous losses in World War I—more than six million casualties—France fell back on a defensive strategy.

The Maginot Line, the most elaborate fortification in military history, was constructed along the Franco-German border. It consisted of interlocking steel and concrete pillboxes, bunkers, strongholds, and tank traps. Underground tunnels equipped with electricity, hot water, air conditioning, and railways linked all sections of the Maginot Line.

In the event of another war with Germany, French strategists reasoned, the enemy would be decimated if he attacked. The French General Staff was smugly confident that their magnificent fortress ensured national security.

But by 1938, the French had begun to worry about the growing power of the Germans. The French Air Force was inadequate by any standards. Strikes and political unrest had disrupted aircraft production while German factories worked around the clock.

In March 1938 the Fuehrer completed an *anschluss*—merger— with Austria. Until 1918, Austria and Germany had been politically united in the powerful Austro-German Empire. The Versailles Treaty had severed those ties. But Hitler could not bear to see his homeland, Austria, independent of the Reich. "Austrians and Germans are brothers!" the Fuehrer declared. "We belong in the same house! One folk! One Reich! One Fuehrer!"

At his prodding, Austrian Nazis stirred up disorders in Linz, Vienna, Innsbruck, and other cities. To "prevent bloodshed, restore order, and protect German interests," Hitler demanded that his troops be permitted to enter Austria. The harassed Austrian government finally gave in; Hitler would have come with or without its consent, and resistance was impossible.

On March 11, 1938, the Wehrmacht goose-stepped over the German-Austrian frontier. The soldiers were followed by agents of terror—the Gestapo (Secret Police), the SS (Elite Troops), and the SA (Storm Troops). It was the end of the short-lived Austrian Republic.

The Nazi dictator's appetite was not yet sated, however. He had his eyes on other territory, primarily the Sudeten district of Czechoslovakia. In that region lived some 3,250,000 Germans Hitler wanted them back in the Fatherland.

CHAPTER 4

The country known as Czechoslovakia had been created in 1918 by the Versailles Treaty. Although it was a new state, Czechoslovakia was an old nation. The Czechs and the Slovaks had been united a thousand years before, during the days of the Moravian Empire. But since that distant time, the Slovaks had been under Hungarian rule, the Czechs under Austrian. With the formation of the Austro-Hungarian Empire in 1878, both nationalities became subjects of Emperor Franz Joseph.

For many years, the Czechs, the Slovaks, and other groups, such as the Magyars and Ruthenians, had been trying to free themselves from the Austro-Hungarian Empire. With the First World War came the chance they had been seeking. The Hapsburg rulers of Austria-Hungary were defeated; the Empire was broken up.

Through the dedicated efforts of Tomas Garrigue Masaryk, son of a Czech coachman and a Slovak maidservant, the demand for an independent Czechoslovak nation was raised. Masaryk was aided in this endeavor by an equally devoted Czech nationalist, Eduard Benes, a man of peasant stock who was educated at the University of Prague and at the Sorbonne in Paris.

Tomas Masaryk became the first President of Czechoslovakia, and Eduard Benes was his foreign minister. In 1935, Masaryk resigned, to be succeeded by Benes.

In the years following its founding Czechoslovakia developed into the most prosperous, democratic, and progressive state of central Europe.

The presence of numerous minorities within the nation's population, however, posed vexsome difficulties from the outset. Among the difficulties was the national minorities question. In the Czechoslovak state were 3,250,000 Sudeten Germans, 1,000,- 000 Hungarians (Magyars), and 500,000 Ruthenians. These groups considered their "homeland" to be Germany, Hungary, and Russia, respectively. The Sudetenlanders had never actually been a part of Germany—but rather of Austria; that made little difference in 1938, however, since Austria and Germany were now reunited.

The chief difficulty plaguing the Czechoslovakian government was that each of the minorities kept demanding autonomy within the framework of the state. The Slovaks, who numbered 1,500,- 000, also wanted more autonomy.

Minorities in Czechoslovakia fared better than those in most countries. None were deprived of civil rights, and to an extent, they had their own native language schools and followed their traditional cultural patterns. But occasionally minority groups suffered mistreatment. Sometimes they were the victims of social and economic discrimination. This was not, however, governmental policy. On the whole, the minorities got along well; the Sudeten Germans, best of all.

The Sudetenlanders lived in the most highly industrialized areas of Czechoslovakia, located along the Republic's northwestern and southwestern frontiers. Jobs were plentiful, and fairly harmonious relations existed between Czechs and the Sudeten people.

Although Sudeten leaders continually pressed the central government in Prague for more autonomy and more German-language schools, no one threatened violence or revolution against Prague. Socialists and other democratic political parties won most elections in Sudetenland.

In 1933, when the Nazis and Adolf Hitler came to power in Germany, the Sudetenland underwent grave changes. Konrad Henlein, formerly a gymnastics teacher, founded a Sudeten Nazi party, and the German Foreign Office secretly provided him with thousands of marks every month to finance Sudeten Nazi activities. Henlein made frequent trips to Berlin, where he consulted with Hitler. His party soon won over most Sudetenlanders; Social Democrats, Communists, and Jews opposed it, but their op-

32

position was ineffectual against Nazi demagoguery and storm troop-style violence.

After annexing Austria, the Fuehrer decided to move against Czechoslovakia. He had ample reason for wanting to take over the prosperous little republic. Annexation would give Germany better frontiers from a military point of view, and the Sudetenland would add another 3,250,000 "Germans," providing the manpower for some ten or twelve Army divisions. Germany would also gain valuable industrial plants, factories, railroads, and highways.

Hitler masked his real purpose—the absorption of Czechoslovakia—by raising demands for only the Sudetenland. The greatest risk in this venture was the chance of provoking war with France, Great Britain, and possibly Russia.

France had a mutual assistance pact with Czechoslovakia. Britain had a military understanding with France. The Soviet Union and France also had a treaty. In addition Czechoslovakia was linked with Rumania and Yugoslavia in the Little Entente, a combination openly aimed at Hungary.

But there were loopholes in all these alliances. The British were obliged to join with France only if the latter were attacked. The Soviet Union had an escape clause in its commitment to France: the Russians had to fight only *after* the French went to war. The Little Entente members were required to act solely in the event that Hungary was the aggressor.

Hitler assessed his chances with a gambler's coolness. He decided that the opposition was not very formidable. The French, torn by internal troubles, would not march, and if France did not move, Russia was not bound to do so. Great Britain was too weak militarily to matter.

The inaction of the Allies when Germany violated the Versailles Treaty, and their feeble protests over the Austrian *anschluss,* convinced Hitler that neither Great Britain nor France were likely to aid Czechoslovakia. If they had not stopped him from retaking the Rhineland two years earlier, when Germany was much weaker, he reasoned, they certainly would not resort to force in 1938.

(Actually, during the occupation of Austria, many flaws in the Wehrmacht had been revealed. More than 70 percent of the Ger-

33

man tanks had broken down because of mechanical defects. Hitler's war machine was impressive, but far from perfect.)

Having decided upon absorbing Czechoslovakia, Hitler gave the signal to activate a secret plan which bore the code name *Fall Grüen* (Case Green), an outline for the conquest of the Czechoslovak Republic.

As a first step toward carrying out Case Green, Konrad Henlein was summoned to Berlin shortly after the annexation of Austria. The Fuehrer told him that "the hour of Sudeten liberation" was at hand, but that Germany could not rescue the Sudetenlanders unless they "helped themselves." He ordered Henlein to "make all the trouble possible," to raise such outlandish demands of the Czechs that Prague could never possibly accept them.

Henlein proceeded to call meetings of the Sudeten Nazi Party which were attended by thousands of his followers. In defiance of Prague, they carried swastika flags and gave the Nazi salute while police stood by without interfering. The Nazis so outnumbered the police that it would have been suicidal for the police to take action. Henlein's uniformed bullies strutted in the streets, breaking the windows of shops owned by anti-Nazis, beating up Jews, setting fires, starting riots.

President Eduard Benes was willing to make reasonable concessions to the Sudeten Germans. He had already offered them more autonomy and a stronger voice in the federal government.

But Benes knew that Germany intended to dominate southeastern Europe, and he wanted to prevent this. If Great Britain and France supported him he would deal with Germany and try to reach a solution that was "manly, dignified, honest, and clear."

Benes would do so, however, only if Great Britain and France guaranteed that any agreement reached with Germany was honored by the Nazis. With the Western Powers behind him, the Czech President promised to fight before letting the Nazis flout the terms of any treaty reached between Czechoslovakia and Germany.

Benes realized that Czechoslovakia would suffer a fate similar to that of Austria unless he could negotiate with the Nazis from a position of strength. A forthright declaration of support from France and Great Britain might bring Hitler up short. Benes and his advisers believed the Fuehrer did not want a war over the Sudetenland.

The thirty-seven-division Czech Army, more than 800,000 well-led, well-trained, well-equipped men, backed by the Western Allies and entrenched within the so-called "Little Maginot Line," located in the northern mountains of Bohemia and Sudetenland, would be no pushover for the Nazis.

If Hitler attacked Czechoslovakia, he would be faced with the prospect of a two-front war. Once the fighting started, Benes firmly believed that all the small countries of central Europe—Yugoslavia, Rumania, Bulgaria, even Hungary—would turn on the Nazis, not so much to defend Czechoslovakia as to protect themselves. In a general conflict, Soviet Russia was not likely to stand aside while there was a chance to defeat the Nazis.

In seeking positive assurances from Great Britain and France, Benes was following what he considered to be a logical course. An isolated Austria had been swallowed up. Benes did not intend to run that risk. He felt that the best insurance against an Austrian-style *anschluss* was a firm understanding with the Western Powers.

Unfortunately, the Czech President erred in staking his country's future on Great Britain and France. Both nations were having second thoughts about their protégé, Czechoslovakia.

In December 1937, a British journalist wrote, "Czechoslovakia is like a child born out of wedlock—unwanted, yet alive and kicking. . . . She is there, we sired her. . . . How we'd love to unburden ourselves of this bundle. . . ."

In the twenty years since the birth of the Czech state, Allied diplomats had learned it was far easier to create a country by changing boundary lines than it was to defend and protect it.

An honest, forthright man, Benes believed the British and French leaders were equally honorable. Without qualms he entrusted Czechoslovakia to the Allies. The awareness that he was surrendering some measure of Czech independence by meshing Prague's foreign policy with that of London and Paris did not disturb him. After all, what benefited Great Britain and France benefited Czechoslovakia—or so he reasoned.

Soon enough, he was to discover his mistake.

35

CHAPTER 5

President Benes badly misinterpreted the political climate in Great Britain and France and overestimated the loyalty of the wartime allies. In London, the government was headed by sixty-nine-year-old Neville Chamberlain, who became Prime Minister on May 28, 1937, succeeding Stanley Baldwin.

Neville Chamberlain's first choice for a career had not been politics. A businessman, he rose to prominence in Birmingham's commercial community. Entering politics at the request of the local Conservative Party in 1911, he was elected to the city council. Within a few years, the tall, austere Chamberlain, who seldom appeared in public without bowler hat and furled umbrella, was elected Lord Mayor of his native city.

During the First World War, Chamberlain served in various economic advisory posts and was elected to Parliament in 1918 at the age of forty-nine.

He soon rose to cabinet rank, gaining distinction in 1924 as minister of health. While holding this post, he established an excellent program of social welfare, including housing provisions, pure food and drug regulations, town planning and national health services. From 1931 until 1937, when he became Prime Minister, he served as chancellor of the exchequer (treasurer). As a cabinet officer, Chamberlain showed himself to be a good administrator with an eye for details which often amazed his colleagues.

Chamberlain was a hardheaded, conservative politician with a shrewd and analytical mind; he could be tough and brusque, especially to those opposing his views. Contrary to popular misconception, he was not a pacifist. Over Laborite objections, he introduced a rearmament bill in the mid-1930s.

His predecessor, Stanley Baldwin, showed little interest in foreign affairs; but Chamberlain had a deep desire to improve the international situation and to establish permanent peace.

He called his peace program "appeasement." This did not mean "peace at any price," he explained, but rather the peaceful solution of problems that might lead to war. The thought of another war was abhorrent to him. In Chamberlain's opinion almost any sacrifice was preferable to a repetition of 1914–18. England would fight, however, if her existence were endangered by an intractable enemy.

One of the major opponents of appeasement was Anthony Eden, the dapper foreign minister, who resigned from office in February 1938 and was replaced by Lord Edward Halifax. Retaining his seat in Parliament, Eden remained a critic of appeasement. Even before Eden's resignation, Chamberlain, impatient at the slow progress made by professional diplomats, had taken control of Britain's foreign policy.

Chamberlain believed that the only way to prevent war was by face-to-face discussions between the heads of governments. The British Prime Minister rejected the general belief that Hitler and his ally, Italy's Duce, Benito Mussolini, would deliberately provoke a world war. Although they blustered and threatened, Chamberlain was convinced that their bellicose attitudes were purely tactics to gain their demands. It was inconceivable to him that any country's leader actually wanted war. The way to prevent a conflict, he thought, was to remove its causes; even Hitler could be made to understand this.

Despite the illogic of coming to a fair settlement with Germany, Chamberlain persisted in the effort. He made the goal of Anglo-German amity a personal, obsessive crusade, and surrounded himself with advisers who had the same delusion.

Among his close associates was Sir Horace Wilson, a career civil servant who had attained high position in government. Wilson was earnest and hard-working, but scarcely qualified to be the Prime Minister's chief consultant on foreign affairs. Also included in Chamberlain's inner circle were Sir Samuel Hoare, the home secretary; Sir John Simon, chancellor of the exchequer; and

Lord Edward Halifax, the foreign minister. Each was a proper British gentleman who shared the Prime Minister's religious, social, political, and international views. Each was dedicated to the principles of appeasement.

Of all his aides, Chamberlain had no more loyal backer than Sir Neville Henderson, the British ambassador to Berlin. Henderson openly avowed his admiration for the Fuehrer and Nazism, and had absolute faith in appeasement as a foundation for lasting peace. In addition, Sir Neville believed that God had given him a divine mission to prevent another world war.

Chamberlain and Henderson were incapable of coping with Nazi aggression. Yet, in many ways, they reflected mass feeling in England.

Most Britons wanted to avoid another war. The British remembered only too well the slaughter of 1914–18. Only a handful of Englishmen protested against Hitler's tyranny; the majority were concerned with "making a go of things" in depression-haunted Britain, where the unemployed daily engaged in a fruitless quest for work and families barely subsisted on a dole handed out grudgingly by a reluctant government.

President Benes realistically could have expected little succor from England in a confrontation with Hitler. But Benes and his colleagues refused to face the fact that Great Britain would surrender Czechoslovakia to the Nazis in the name of appeasement.

The French were, if possible, even less inclined to fight than the British. The Popular Front government led by Premier Léon Blum consisted of a flimsy coalition of political parties that included moderates, Socialists, Communists, and Liberals.

Blum, a veteran Socialist, was unhappy about the threat facing the Czechs but could do nothing about it. His government remained in power by a frayed thread, which threatened to snap at any time. Blum was finally toppled from office on April 8, 1938.

The man who succeeded Blum as Premier was Edouard Daladier, who had held posts in a dozen cabinets, and twice before had been Premier. Daladier was born in 1884 at Carpentras in the department of the Vaucluse. The son of a baker, he studied to become a history professor and was teaching that subject at a university when World War I broke out. Entering the Army, he was soon promoted to sergeant. For bravery in action, Daladier won the Legion of Honor, the *Croix de guerre,* three citations, and a battlefield commission as captain.

In 1918, the much-decorated war hero tried his hand at politics and won a seat in the Chamber of Deputies as a representative from the Vaucluse, a position he held for twenty years.

His first premiership came in 1933. Daladier lasted nine months in office—a near-record at a time when French cabinets were falling like leaves in autumn. He became Premier again in January 1934. This time his government fell after only a month in the wake of Fascist-inspired riots that turned Paris and other cities into battlegrounds.

When the Popular Front government was elected in 1936, Daladier offered to serve in Premier Blum's cabinet, deserting his old party, the Radical Socialists, who were shunning the Popular Front. Blum rewarded Daladier's defection by appointing him minister of war.

Edouard Daladier was no great statesman, but he was an able politician who knew how to shift with the popular tide. A stocky, big-shouldered man, Daladier had been nicknamed the "Bull of the Vaucluse" by his colleagues in the Chamber of Deputies. If he lacked qualities of leadership, Daladier had one outstanding virtue: he was completely honest in financial affairs, a mark of distinction among French political figures in the 1930s. At times he was willing to forego principles to gain votes, however.

In selecting a foreign minister for his 1938 cabinet, Daladier chose expedience over integrity. Joseph Paul-Boncour, the incumbent, had strong ideas about central Europe, particularly the security of Czechoslovakia. Daladier knew that many Deputies disagreed with Paul-Boncour's position, which was to state France's unequivocal support of the Czechoslovaks.

Such forthrightness was politically unwise in Daladier's opinion; the matter might come to a vote in the Chamber of Deputies and result in the government's downfall.

The "Bull of the Vaucluse" did not choose to run that risk. He dropped Paul-Boncour, an excellent foreign minister, and replaced him with Georges Bonnet, who was once characterized by a political observer as "a cagey careerist who would not discuss the weather unless a poll was first taken so he might judge the feelings of the majority. . . ."

A vain and ambitious man with dreams of someday being Premier, Bonnet had taken no stand on Czechoslovakia, which suited Daladier's purposes.

Once in office, Bonnet hastened to assure Stefan Osusky, the Czechoslovak ambassador to Paris, that the departure of Paul-Boncour changed nothing in France's relationship with Czechoslovakia. Bonnet hedged skillfully on the question of French support, however. Osusky had to be satisfied with ambiguous policy statements such as "France would not compromise her honor," and "France has always answered the call when democracy was threatened."

While these phrases gave small comfort to the Czechoslovaks, Benes had no choice but to go along with France in the hope that Bonnet meant what he said.

Actually Georges Bonnet had no intention of taking France into a war against Germany on behalf of Czechoslovakia—treaty or no treaty. France, he declared, was ready to march—if the British would also do so. This was a safe position. Bonnet knew that Chamberlain's government would yield to Hitler on the Czech question rather than go to war. If Britain backed down, then France certainly could not be expected to fight Hitler alone. The responsibility of abandoning Czechoslovakia would fall upon the British.

No doubt some Czechoslovak leaders were dubious of British support; but none believed France would fail to honor the mutual aid treaty between the two countries. Perhaps if the Czechoslovaks had not so desperately wished for help from the west, they might have been able to make an objective estimate of their French ally.

Opposition to war was as widespread in France as it was in Britain, but differences in public attitude existed. In France, universal conscription was practiced; Britain had no draft. Since every physically fit Frenchman was obliged to serve in the Army, the military establishment was close to all levels of French society. A journalist wrote: "In France, the army is the people and the people are the army. . . ."

Many Frenchmen felt a deep-rooted hatred and fear of the Germans, who had spread devastation across France in two wars —1870–71 and 1914–18. But a government leading France into a

41

costly conflict with Germany merely to save the Czechoslovaks from Hitler was likely to be tossed out of office.

Ironically, a number of right-wing Frenchmen sympathized with the Nazis. France had been sold out, the Gallic Fascists shouted. The nation was being ruined by Jews, Bolsheviks, and "international bankers." Fascist groups, whose membership included Army officers, called for an end to "Jew-dominated republicanism" and a return to *la gloire*—the days of French glory under a king or an emperor.

Bloody rioting often erupted in major French cities as left-wingers battled Fascists. The country lacked political unity; a major upheaval, such as a war, might end in revolution—either from the left or the right.

In 1938, as the new crisis in central Europe took shape, an American commentator noted in a newspaper column, "No man can predict what the next few weeks or months will bring in Europe. . . . Perhaps some clue may lie in the announcement that Lloyd's of London, which has issued insurance policies to cover any imaginable situation, has refused to insure against the outbreak of a general European war. . . ."

CHAPTER 6

Adolf Hitler was a man of uncertain temper. He could fly into fits of uncontrolled rage with little provocation. Whether these outbursts were staged by him to get what he wanted, or whether they indicated some form of madness, they sometimes proved useful. To achieve his ends, Hitler would employ whatever means seemed likely to succeed—cajolery, frenzy, or brute force. The Fuehrer often stated his credo: "If I believe in my cause, if it benefits the Fatherland, I will cheat, lie, steal, kill. The end justifies the means; there is no such thing as morality where the well-being of my country and my people is involved. . . ."

Hitler was a practitioner of the Big Lie: "If you repeat something often enough, with forceful conviction, you can make it seem more truthful than truth itself," he wrote in *Mein Kampf*. By such means he convinced the German people that all their troubles stemmed from Jews, Communists, trade unionists, liberals, and democrats. For every unpleasant reality Hitler substituted a skillfully fabricated delusion.

As Case Green became operative, he brought this technique into play once more. In a moment of candor, Hitler had revealed to his aides the real goal of Case Green: "It is my unshakable will that Czechoslovakia shall be wiped off the map!" he thundered.

The Fuehrer realized that Germany could more easily attain her goals in central Europe if several other nations joined the assault upon Czechoslovakia. He started working on this early in 1938 when he indicated to Hungarian officials visiting Berlin that, one day, Czechoslovakia might become a German objective. Generously, he offered Hungary the eastern half of that country after the conquest.

The Yugoslavian Premier, Milan Stoyadinovitch, was wooed by high-ranking Nazis who exacted from him the promise that, during his regime, at least, Yugoslavia would never enter into any pact against Germany. In similar fashion, the Germans undermined the Little Entente, promising territorial favors to both Rumania and Yugoslavia.

One country after another indicated support of the Nazi plans against Czechoslovakia. Bulgaria's King Boris III, referring to the Czechoslovaks as the "Jews among the Slavs," stated that he did not care a "grain of wheat" over Czechoslovakia's fate.

The nation most likely to be adversely affected by a Nazi victory in the Czechoslovak-Sudeten crisis was Poland. But Polish leaders foolishly believed they could benefit from a Czechoslovak defeat. Motivated by greed, nationalism, and blind hatred, the Poles, led by Foreign Minister Joseph Beck, played the Nazi game because Hitler shrewdly dangled a region called Teschen before them.

Teschen, located in Silesia, had once belonged to Poland but was taken by Czechoslovakia in 1920, while the Poles were fighting the Bolsheviks. The area had little strategic value to Poland, but was an important rail and road center for the Czechoslovaks. Only 120,000 Poles lived in Teschen under Czech rule; bringing them home to Poland made little difference to that nation, but the territorial loss would mean serious difficulty for Czechoslovakia.

Tall, elegant Colonel Joseph Beck ran his country's foreign affairs with a dictatorial hand. When the Czechoslovak-Sudeten crisis began to flare, the colonel made it clear that under no circumstances would Poland allow Russian troops across her territory to aid the Czechoslovaks; nor could Russian planes fly over Poland.

His hatred of Czechoslovakia and Russia so blinded Beck that he saw only the immediate result of a Czechoslovak debacle: an opportunity for Poland to regain the Teschen district. Beck and his countrymen were to learn that those who accepted Hitler's bounty could not escape his domination.

To the rest of the world, Hitler announced that his sole concern in Czechoslovakia was the fate of the 3,500,000 Sudeten German "blood brothers" now being maltreated by the Czechoslovaks.

This smokescreen even misled some of the leaders of Czechoslovakia. Milan Hodza, the Czechoslovak Prime Minister, was one of those taken in by Hitler's assertion that the Sudetenland and the condition of the German minority there comprised the only problem between Germany and Czechoslovakia.

At a meeting with Ernst Eisenlohr, the German ambassador to Prague, on March 23, 1938, Hodza offered a settlement of the Sudeten question. The Prime Minister volunteered sweeping concessions: the Sudeten German Party would be invited to enter the government; all followers of Henlein who had been imprisoned were to be set free under an amnesty; Sudetenlanders would be exempt from military service; German-language schools would be increased in the Sudeten area.

In return for this, Hodza asked that the Sudeten German Party renounce violence and adopt democratic methods. If this were done, the Prime Minister promised, Henlein's followers could profess any ideology they desired, fly swastika flags, wear uniforms or identifying badges, and hold meetings without interference from the Prague government. The Sudeten Germans must not persecute anyone for religious or political reasons, however.

Eisenlohr, making no comment, agreed to pass Hodza's proposals on to Berlin. The German ambassador may have done so, but nothing concrete developed. Street clashes between Czechoslovaks and Sudetenlanders continued.

Soon after his conference with Eisenlohr, the Prime Minister called in Sudeten leaders to conduct negotiations for a "peaceable and permanent settlement" between Prague and the Sudeten minority. These sessions proved fruitless. Every time it appeared that an area of agreement had been reached, the Sudeten representatives issued another demand.

"If the talks had gone on long enough," a Hodza aide confided to an American newspaperman, "Henlein's bunch would have asked for the world and even that wouldn't have satisfied them."

Obviously, the Sudeten Nazis were complying with Hitler's orders to make demands which were impossible for the Czechoslovaks to accept. Meanwhile, Hitler perfected Case Green. By

April 21, he had prepared an initial directive for the projected attack on Czechoslovakia.

In this draft, the Fuehrer pointed out that the groundwork must be properly laid for the invasion of the Czechoslovak Republic. The German attack had to have proper motivation. Hitler suggested that Nazi stooges in Prague stage a violent demonstration outside the German Embassy. During the course of the riot, hand-picked Nazi gunmen would kill a German diplomat—Ernst Eisenlohr, if possible; otherwise, a minor embassy attaché would do.

Who then could blame Germany for taking revenge on the murderers of their ambassador? Surely world opinion would sympathize with the Germans.

Since this was to be his first aggression against a completely foreign nation which had no historical, cultural, or political ties with Germany, the Fuehrer wanted to make it appear that the Czechoslovaks, not the Germans, had incited the conflict.

Hitler's suggestion of a phony demonstration followed by the slaying of a Nazi official won the enthusiastic approval of General Wilhelm Keitel, Chief of the Supreme Command of the Wehrmacht.

Keitel, long a Hitler toady, would have applauded any idea put forth by the Fuehrer. In fact, all the officers who were made privy to the directive on Case Green warmly accepted Hitler's scheme. Ernst Eisenlohr, faithfully carrying out his duties in Prague, knew nothing of the reward the Fuehrer was readying for him.

The Case Green directive also stressed the need for an opening assault of overwhelming force. The attack had to be launched at many points along the frontier, by land and by air. It had to be capable of crushing Czechoslovak resistance swiftly and ruthlessly.

"Gentlemen," Hitler told Keitel and staff, "I am speaking of total war, lightning war, *blitzkrieg!* We must hit first and smash the foe's will in a few days—but the victory will be won in the opening hours. *Blitzkrieg,* gentlemen, *blitzkrieg!* Lightning war!"

To allay international suspicions of his intention to destroy Czechoslovakia, Hitler continued the pretense of deep concern over the plight of the Sudetenlanders.

The Fuehrer's propaganda chief, Joseph Goebbels, an adept practitioner of the Big Lie, used press and radio to spread fabricated tales of Czechoslovak atrocities against innocent Sudetenlanders. Goebbels cried out bitterly against the "bestial treatment" being accorded German "kinsmen" in Czechoslovakia.

While Goebbels expertly whipped up anti-Czechoslovak sentiment among the German people, Konrad Henlein and his followers inflamed the Sudetenlanders, calling upon them to rise against their Czechoslovak "oppressors."

For reasons still unknown, Chamberlain and Daladier chose to swallow the Nazi propaganda about terror in Sudetenland and to disbelieve Czechoslovak denials. As spring came to Europe, the British and French pressed the Czechoslovaks to grant far-reaching concessions to the Sudeten Germans. But no matter how Prague tried to appease Henlein, he always demanded more. And no matter how much Henlein asked, Britain and France urged the Czechoslovaks to satisfy him.

The British were more persistent in this than the French. Sir Basil Newton, Britain's ambassador to Prague, advised Prime Minister Chamberlain that rendering any assistance to Czechoslovakia was "fruitless." Germany was going to take over the Czechoslovak Republic and would go to war to accomplish this purpose. Even if Britain and France supported the Czechoslovaks, "nothing could keep the Germans from overrunning Czechoslovakia." The only course for Britain to follow, according to Sir Basil, was to let Hitler have his way.

Sir Neville Henderson, who characterized Hitler as a "constructive genius," felt that Germany should be allowed to dominate the regions east of the Rhine all the way to the Russian frontier. According to him, once Hitler settled the Sudeten problem and readjusted Germany's eastern borders, the Fuehrer would have no further territorial demands in Europe. Henderson argued that these concessions to Hitler were necessary to maintain peace. "I believe the German demands are just," he said. "The Versailles Treaty was written to degrade and humiliate a proud nation. . . . We must do our best to rectify twenty years of unnecessary hardships inflicted on Germany. . . ."

With such opinions prevailing in British governmental circles, Premier Daladier of France dared not commit his country to honor the Czechoslovak treaty.

Matters reached a climax on April 24, at Karlsbad, in western

Bohemia, a Sudeten German stronghold. The occasion was the Sudeten Nazi Party's Congress, which was attended by thousands of uniformed Party members who came to hear their leader, Konrad Henlein, present a new set of demands to Prague.

Henlein told his cheering audience that he was willing to make a peaceable settlement of the Sudeten question, but the terms he offered were steep.

If the Sudetenlanders were to remain within the Czechoslovak nation, Henlein said, they no longer would tolerate being considered a minority. The Sudeten Germans looked toward the Third Reich as their Fatherland—not Czechoslovakia.

If Prague granted all his terms, however, the Sudeten people were willing to retain Czechoslovak citizenship. Henlein then presented demands which called for a virtual reconstruction of the Czechoslovak nation:

1. The Sudeten Germans must be recognized as a legal entity.

2. They must have equality in rights and status with the Czechoslovak people.

3. The Sudeten area must have complete autonomy and a separate government.

4. Only German officials could hold office in regions dominated by a Sudeten German population.

5. Sudeten Germans living outside the autonomous area must be guaranteed full legal, civil, and economic rights.

6. All injustices and inequalities suffered by the Sudetenlanders since 1918 must be remedied.

7. Prague must pay monetary reparations to all Sudeten Germans who have suffered past mistreatment.

8. The Sudeten Germans must be permitted to follow and practice, within their areas, the Nazi ideology.

Even as he put forth his eight conditions, Henlein knew the Czechoslovak government could not accept them. It would have been intolerable for President Benes to allow the creation within the Czechoslovak state of a separate state owing allegiance to a foreign power and posing a continuing threat to the security of the entire country.

48

Further, Benes and his colleagues were not so naïve as to believe that the Karlsbad demands ended Henlein's ambitions. They were an impossible basis for negotiations because the Sudeten Nazi leader would have pressed for further concessions had he won these.

The Czechoslovak government neither rejected nor accepted the Karlsbad demands; instead it sought to continue negotiations on a more practicable level. In the meantime, an order went out to all police chiefs not to interfere with Nazi meetings, demonstrations, or other activities unless they became dangerous to "life, limb, or property."

Prime Minister Chamberlain reacted to Henlein's eight demands by inviting the new French Premier, Edouard Daladier, whom he had never met, to London for a top-level conference. Daladier accepted and came to the British capital on April 27, accompanied by his foreign minister, Georges Bonnet.

CHAPTER 7

According to schedule, the Franco-British conference was supposed to convene at 10:30 A.M., Thursday, April 28, at No. 10 Downing Street, the official residence of Britain's prime ministers. Just before the appointed time, Premier Daladier, a heavy smoker, found that he was out of cigarettes. Although offered various brands of British cigarettes, Daladier insisted on his favorite kind, *Gauloises*, a strong French cigarette.

Prime Minister Chamberlain was annoyed at the delay, but sought to satisfy his guest's whim. An orderly was sent out to buy *Gauloises*. It took him almost an hour to locate a tobacconist who sold the brand.

When the meeting finally got under way, Chamberlain bluntly informed Daladier that France would get very little help from Great Britain in a war with Germany.

The best the French could hope for was two underequipped British divisions and a few Royal Air Force (RAF) fighters and bombers. Chamberlain then expounded at length on his country's feeble military condition. He suggested to Daladier that France avoid war if she needed British aid. Chamberlain also stressed that British obligations to France were limited to the terms of the 1925 Locarno Treaty.

Under this agreement, Britain guaranteed both the Belgian-German and the Franco-German frontiers. The Locarno Treaty did not provide for the Czechoslovakian situation. It was questionable whether Great Britain was bound to fight over such an issue unless the Germans crossed the French border. (In 1935,

51

Belgium had canceled her role in the Locarno Treaty, accepted a guarantee from Germany, and declared neutrality.)

When the first day's session adjourned, gloom hung heavily over the French delegation. It was apparent that France must either extricate herself from the Czechoslovak pact or else face the possibility of having to fight the Nazis without an ally. The trick was to abandon Czechoslovakia without sacrificing French honor.

Daladier and his colleagues, realizing that this was virtually impossible, decided to attempt to convince the British that the Nazis were a threat not only to Czechoslovakia, but to all of Europe as well. Hitler must be stopped at the borders of Czechoslovakia, the French insisted; he would not be satisfied with the Sudetenland, but would demand more and more, until Germany dominated the continent.

The meeting resumed on Friday, April 29. At the gavel, the British foreign minister, Lord Halifax, further dampened prospects of joint Franco-British action on behalf of Czechoslovakia.

According to him, the Czechoslovak situation was made hopeless by the military weaknesses of Britain, France, and Czechoslovakia. Therefore, the only logical policy for the Allies was to urge Benes to make a "supreme effort" to reach a settlement of the Sudeten issue. Halifax further argued that even if Germany were defeated in a war, Czechoslovakia could not continue in its present form.

The mistake had been made in 1918, he said; there was no need to compound it in 1938. "We shall have to learn to live with the reality that the Czech nation no longer can exist as originally conceived. . . . The Sudeten problem must be solved without resort to arms. . . . It is a hollow cause at best. . . ."

In his reply to Halifax, Premier Daladier revealed himself as a man of courage and honor. Daladier argued that Czechoslovakia must not be "left to drown" because of her "imperfections." No nation was perfect, no nation was pure. "For twenty years," Daladier said, "the Czechoslovak Republic has been a bulwark of democracy where autocrats once ruled. . . . The danger does not lie in the Sudetenland . . . it lies beyond. . . . Hitler is a madman bent on conquest. . . . He must be halted in his tracks, now!"

Daladier did not overlook the chances of a peaceable solution to the crisis, however. The Czechoslovaks, he agreed, must make the "supreme effort" Halifax had suggested. But what if it were turned down by Henlein? What if Germany marched? It was incumbent on Great Britain and France to preserve the independence of small nations. According to French intelligence reports, Hitler intended to absorb Czechoslovakia as he had absorbed Austria.

It was one thing for Hitler to back the German minority in Czechoslovakia and quite another to swallow up an independent nation. France would never let this happen. She would honor her treaty with Czechoslovakia—hopefully with Britain at her side, alone if necessary.

Daladier had intended to move Chamberlain with a display of boldness, but failed in his purpose. The Prime Minister clung to the position that the combined forces of France and Great Britain were not strong enough to save Czechoslovakia. The British public, Chamberlain averred, would "throw out of office" any government that led them to war for the Czechoslovaks.

Back and forth the discussion swung, Daladier and Bonnet insisting that their country would support Czechoslovakia, "come what may," the British refusing to budge.

As the day waned, Daladier and Bonnet grew convinced that Chamberlain and Halifax meant what they said. Once the Frenchmen saw that Britain could not be tied down to any positive commitments, they backed off and accepted the British position.

It was agreed that Chamberlain's government would advise Berlin that it wanted a peaceable solution to the Sudeten controversy. Prague would be counseled to make all necessary compromises. The British would assure Hitler that there was no need for German involvement. Britain and France would secure every possible concession for the Sudetenlanders. The Germans would also be told, however, that should a peaceful solution prove impossible, and it became necessary for France to help the Czechoslovaks, Britain could not guarantee "to remain an observer of the conflict."

This was the best Daladier could get from Chamberlain; the British Prime Minister would not go beyond this vague promise.

Once it had been made clear that Britain could not be counted on in the event of war, Daladier no longer spoke of opposing the Nazis with force. He was not willing to subject France to the full brunt of a German attack. Furthermore, such a stance would be political suicide, and Daladier had no wish to become a martyr to the Czechoslovak cause.

The prudent course was to go along with Chamberlain and let the British take the lead in ironing out the Czechoslovak crisis. If recriminations rose over the appeasement of Hitler, Daladier could excuse his actions by pointing out Chamberlain's failure to back him.

Daladier had gone to London in an optimistic mood, believing strong links would be forged between France and Great Britain. From that point of view the meeting was a complete failure.

On his return to Paris, any illusions Daladier might have retained about defending the Czechoslovaks were dissipated. He asked the Chief of Staff, General Maurice Gamelin, for a report on possible military action against Germany if the Czechoslovak crisis caused a war, and received a discouraging response.

Gamelin was more politician than soldier. Instead of the incisive statement Daladier needed, Gamelin offered a rambling, uncertain account. It would be unwise for the French Army to attack the Germans, Gamelin told the Premier. "In this situation," he said, "the best offense is to remain on the defensive. Let the Germans break against the Maginot Line. . . ."

When questioned about what the French would do if the Germans refused to attack, Gamelin again avoided a direct reply. "It is something I will handle when the event arises. . . . Most probably the armies will sit behind their fortifications and glare at each other across the frontier . . . ," he said.

Daladier pointed out that such tactics would not be of much use to the Czechoslovaks. Gamelin agreed. "The main thing is that France will have honored her treaty, kept her word. . . . That is all we should care about. . . . Let Russia, Rumania, Poland, Yugoslavia, and Great Britain do their part. . . . They too, should care about the fate of Czechoslovakia. . . ."

Daladier did not need General Gamelin to remind him that neither Great Britain nor the Little Entente had faced up to their responsibilities toward Czechoslovakia. Had they done so, the French would not be at an impasse; not even Hitler would have dared threaten a united front of small nations backed by Great Britain and France. Unhappily, France was the only country that had evinced the slightest desire to protect Czechoslovakia.

French aircraft production records, when compared to those of the Germans, made the outlook even more dismal. The French Air Force, once the world's best, was hopelessly outclassed by the Luftwaffe.

As far as Daladier was concerned, the curtain had fallen for the Czechoslovaks. Asked by William C. Bullitt, the U. S. ambassador to France, whether he had decided to fight if the Germans attacked Czechoslovakia, Daladier shrugged and said, "Fight? With what?"

Daladier remained pessimistic about the prospects of avoiding war. He freely predicted that before the end of the summer, Germany would provoke a conflict—if not over Czechoslovakia, then over another issue—Danzig, the Polish corridor, Memel, one excuse or another. Perhaps Hitler might even revive the old German dream of the *Drang nach Osten* (Drive to the East)—into the fertile farmlands of the Ukraine, the Russian oilfields, the wide plains where a crowded Germany could find *lebensraum* (living space).

Daladier realized that he no longer controlled his country's foreign policy, having tied France to Great Britain. War or peace would be decided by Neville Chamberlain. It saddened Daladier that France was now in a dependent position. But survival came before principle. This was the politician's creed, and if nothing else, Edouard Daladier was a splendid politician.

His qualms were not shared by Georges Bonnet. The ambitious foreign minister was secretly delighted over the British refusal to back France in support of the Czechoslovaks. To Bonnet, Czechoslovakia was, and always had been, "a motley of minorities and conflicting interests. . . ." He never believed France should have committed herself to the defense of Czechoslovakia.

In a meeting with the Czechoslovak minister in Paris, Stefan Osusky, however, Bonnet declared himself a "stanch friend of Czechoslovakia" and pledged to do all in his power for the "preservation of Czechoslovak freedom and independence." Still, Bonnet urged Osusky to use every influence on Benes for a settlement of the Sudeten trouble. No one profited from a war, he argued. If fighting broke out, Czechoslovakia would be a battlefield. "France knows the meaning of war on her soil. Spare your country from such horror; what good is national honor if your land lies ruined and devastated?" he told Osusky.

After leaving the Czechoslovak minister, Bonnet called upon the German ambassador. To him, the wily Frenchman sang a different song. He tried to convince the German that the conference in London had not been aimed against the Reich. On the contrary, Bonnet explained, Britain and France had explored all avenues for satisfying Germany.

Bonnet assured the ambassador of his "admiration for the rise and achievements of the New Germany which, after the incorporation of Austria, had so splendid and varied a reconstruction program before it. . . ."

He begged Germany not to force France to honor her alliance with the Czechoslovaks. "The Sudeten area is not worth a single French or German life," Bonnet argued. "Both Britain and France will work to settle your demands in a manner pleasing to Germany. . . . Truly, any arrangement is better than a war in which all Europe—victors and vanquished alike—would perish. . . ."

At about the same time Chamberlain's foreign minister, Lord Halifax, was attempting to undermine Czechoslovak confidence. On May 2, he told Jan Masaryk, Czechoslovakia's ambassador and the son of the nation's first President, that it would be futile to meet the Germans with force. The Wehrmacht and the Luftwaffe would crush Czechoslovak resistance long before any French and British help could come. Besides, he warned, Great Britain might not choose to enter the war. It was far wiser for the Czechoslovaks to yield on the Sudeten issue. Britain was willing to lend her good offices as a mediator between Germany and Czechoslovakia.

And so in the early days of May 1938, the pressure on the Czechoslovaks constantly increased. Urged to give in by both allies and fearful colleagues, President Eduard Benes remained firm. He refused to see Henlein, as the British insisted, if the meeting was to discuss autonomy for the Sudetenland. Benes knew that should the Sudeten Germans be given self-government, Prague's authority in the region was finished. The country's main fortification line had been built in the Sudetenland to guard the frontier, and these defenses would have to be abandoned in an autonomous region, a step that would leave Czechoslovakia vulnerable to invasion.

Since Hitler already controlled Austria, he could now attack the Czechoslovaks from three sides simultaneously, forcing them to abandon the outflanked Sudeten fortifications. But this would come only after hard fighting. The Czechoslovak Army was not going to abandon its strongest points of defense without making the enemy pay a high price for them, and Hitler was well aware of this. The safest course for the Fuehrer was to try to win the Sudetenland at the bargaining table, while threatening to wage war for it.

On May 17, the Czechoslovak President met with the British ambassador, Sir Basil Newton. Angrily but with dignity, Benes told Newton, "British policy is an acceptance of German domination of my country. . . . You would make Czechoslovakia a German puppet state. . . .

"You and the French are making a cruel mistake. German domination of Czechoslovakia is only the first step toward their domination of Europe. . . . I warn you, Sir Basil, that the future of Britain and France rests upon what you do in Czechoslovakia. Whether you like it or not—our fate is your fate. Whether you like it or not we shall still cry out for help from the west, even with our last breath of life. . . ."

No matter how Britain and France tried to shake him loose, Benes clung to them for protection. "The Czechoslovaks ride upon our shoulders as the Old Man of the Sea rode upon Sinbad the Sailor's," a British Foreign Office official confided to an American newspaperman.

Sensing that the British were more willing than anyone else to make a deal on the Sudeten issue, Hitler secretly advised Henlein to visit London and lay his case before government officials and other prominent Englishmen.

In London, Henlein described the "pitiable" condition of the Sudetenlanders, swore that his Karlsbad demands would end the trouble, and vowed that he was not under Hitler's orders.

The Prague government, he said, was "playing with fire" by mistreating the Sudeten Germans. Would Englishmen stand idly by and watch the persecution of their kinsmen in a foreign land, he asked? Well, the Reich Germans could do no less.

Henlein urged the British to find a quick solution, otherwise his own followers would revolt against Prague and seek *anschluss* with Germany. Personally, he preferred conciliation with Prague, but the situation was growing out of hand. The choice was Sudeten autonomy or revolution and *anschluss*.

The Sudeten leader impressed some high-ranking Britons, who regarded him as a "sincere, honest and independent man" and not under Hitler's "influence." Winston Churchill, however, was not fooled. "Henlein stood before me, but the voice was the voice of the Bavarian corporal who now rules Germany," Churchill declared. "We do not deserve to be called Englishmen if we truckle to such people. . . ." But in 1938, Neville Chamberlain made Britain's policy, not Winston Churchill. The latter was only a member of Parliament, and had little influence in the government.

CHAPTER 8

By mid-May daily violence between Nazis and Czechoslovak policemen and soldiers was commonplace. Brawls broke out in cafes, restaurants, and on the streets. Sometimes knives flashed and revolvers cracked; participants were wounded and, occasionally, killed in these vicious skirmishes. The day-to-day governing of the Sudeten districts was becoming an almost impossible task for the Czechoslovaks.

Every incident brought an angry response from the Nazis—outcries of "persecution!" and "tyranny!" The Czechoslovaks, on the other hand, demanded that sterner repressive measures be taken against the Sudeten Germans; some newspapers advocated martial law, and the most extreme called for the death penalty for Sudeten Nazis who engaged in "insurrectionary activities."

Henlein's followers began to prepare for an uprising. A guerrilla force, armed with German weapons, was formed to "protect Sudeten life and property" from attack by the "Czech oppressors." This so-called "Free Corps" consisted of hoodlums and criminals who terrorized Jews, Czechoslovaks, and all anti-Nazis in the name of "liberty."

For self-protection, Czechoslovaks living in the Sudeten region armed themselves; few people ventured out at any time of the day or night without a shotgun, pistol, knife, or stout walking stick.

A Swedish journalist, reporting from the Sudetenland, observed: "The threat of civil war hangs heavily; and worse than civil strife is the menace of the Wehrmacht poised across the border. The Sudetenland is a time bomb, and as the clock ticks on, one feels that the moment of explosion is at hand. . . ."

59

On Tuesday, May 17, in the northern Bohemian town of Treb-nitz, members of a German *turnverein* (gymnastic club) suddenly rushed through the main street shouting *"Heil* Henlein! *Heil* Hit-ler! Death to the Czechs!"* As the demonstrators milled about, yelling, cursing, heaving rocks and stones through the windows of homes and shops, armed Free Corps men poured in behind them.

The population of Trebnitz was preponderantly Czechoslovak, and the townspeople rallied to drive off the Nazis. A pitched battle took place and lasted until daybreak when a contingent of riot po-lice and Czechoslovak troops finally broke up the melee. Several Free Corps members were barely saved by police from lynching at the hands of enraged residents.

For the next two days and nights, rioting erupted in several other towns. The violence spread to Prague on Thursday, May 19, when Henleinists carrying swastika flags, tried to parade through the business district.

At the height of the disorders, upsetting rumors reached the Czechoslovak capital; German troops were reportedly massing on the Czech-German and the Czech-Austrian frontiers. By that eve-ning, accounts of German military movements came in from all quarters. German officials scoffed at these reports when queried by British, French, and Czechoslovak diplomats. In Berlin, Sir Nev-ille Henderson was assured by Ernst von Weiszacker, a ranking secretary in the German Foreign Office, that "This talk of Wehr-macht concentrations on the Czechoslovak frontier is sheer non-sense, inspired, no doubt, by Prague propagandists."

Vojtech Mastny, Czechoslovak minister at Berlin, confronted Weiszacker early on Friday, May 20, with charges that not only were units of the Wehrmacht marching to the Czechoslovak bor-ders but also that SS and SA units had been ordered to follow on May 21–22. Weiszacker flatly denied this as "pure poppycock."

Later that evening Mastny called upon German Foreign Minis-ter Joachim von Ribbentrop and posed the question about troop concentrations. Ribbentrop, losing his diplomatic aplomb, shouted an angry denial. "This is a Czech provocation! A dirty, under-handed attempt to smear Germany! You Czechs are looking for a reason to mobilize so you can massacre Sudetenlanders! Try it! Then you will learn what German mobilization means! When we march, you'll *know* it!"

German denials to the contrary, Prague became increasingly distressed about the rumors. The government feared that an attack would come at any moment.

The Czechoslovak General Staff received a flow of intelligence reports concerning military traffic in Germany and Austria. They concluded that this was a prelude to invasion and that the alternatives to such a threat were to accept the fate of Austria or else prepare for a fight.

On the evening of May 20, the Czechoslovak Cabinet held an emergency session. An immediate mobilization order seemed the only suitable response to the Nazis. Obviously, the Germans were trying to intimidate the Czechoslovak government to meet Henlein's demands.

By 9:00 P.M. the cabinet had agreed to call out about 174,000 reservists for duty in Sudetenland; no mention was made of the German threat; men were being called to the colors "to preserve law and order in regions where subversive and insurrectionary acts have occurred. . . ."

All through the night of May 20–21, special trains carrying uniformed Czechoslovak reservists rolled through Prague's central railroad station. By dawn, Army patrols appeared in the streets of Sudeten towns. Henlein's Free Corps made themselves scarce. Swastika flags and Nazi placards vanished.

The inhabitants of one Sudeten town, however, awakened by the clatter of tanks, rushed from their houses, waving swastika flags, in the mistaken belief that German troops were coming to "liberate" them. Their jubilation quickly ended when government soldiers confiscated the banners and arrested some overanxious Nazis.

Near-panic swept Europe when word of the Czechoslovak mobilization reached the capitals. Never since 1914 had war seemed so imminent. There was feverish activity in London, Paris, Moscow, Berlin, and in distant Washington. Telephones jangled, radio messages crackled, telegraph keys clicked. Diplomats dashed from embassy to embassy, seeking information, giving advice, worrying that the long-dreaded conflict was about to begin.

With Czechoslovak troops in the Sudetenland, there were no riots on May 21. Nor could there be a surprise German attack now that the Czechoslovak Army was on the alert. "There will be no *anschluss* here," an Army officer said. "We are not Austrians!"

61

The mobilization, which caught the Sudeten Nazis off guard, gave Henlein an unexpected propaganda bonus. Shortly after daybreak on May 21, two young Sudeten Nazis—George Hoffmann and Nicholas Boehm—were traveling on motorcycles from the town of Cheb to Franzensbad.

Both men had been out all night drinking with Free Corps comrades, and their machines swerved drunkenly as they raced along the dirt road. Just beyond Cheb the Army had set up a roadblock, and the Nazis were signaled to halt. Instead, Hoffmann and Boehm raced through at top speed. The soldiers on duty ordered them to halt in Czechoslovak and in German; when the command was ignored, the sentries opened fire. Hoffmann and Boehm were mortally wounded and died shortly afterward.

The Nazi press had a field day with this story. The headlines shrieked, "Innocent Cyclists Slain by Czech Murderers!" "German Blood Spilled By Czech Butchers!" Memorial services for the "martyrs" were held on the German side of the border; Nazi speakers harangued the crowd, vowing to avenge their "noble sacrifice."

Saturday and Sunday passed without a German attack. But those forty-eight anxious hours, which came to be called the May Crisis, stirred both Britain and France to a more determined stand than they had taken since the onset of the Sudeten problem. Once war actually seemed upon them, the Allies stiffened.

On May 21, Sir Neville Henderson, in Berlin, under instructions from London, told Von Ribbentrop, "The British government have the assurances of the Czechoslovak government that all would be done to obtain a peaceable and just settlement of the Sudeten question. . . . Should a conflict arise . . . France would be compelled to intervene under her obligations toward Czechoslovakia. . . . In such circumstances . . . His Majesty's government could not guarantee that they would not be forced by circumstances to become involved also. . . ."

While this was hardly the strongest possible statement, it marked a change in the British attitude. Foreign Minister von Ribbentrop, to whom Henderson had read the instructions, cynically replied, "The answer to war or peace lies in Prague and Paris —not here. . . . Do as you choose, but you and the French will regret your hostility to Germany. . . ."

62

Henderson hastened to mollify Von Ribbentrop. Personally, he agreed with the German position and hoped that the crisis would be settled without war. "All will be well in the end," Henderson said, "and Germany will win all along the line. After all, this statement is based upon a hypothetical situation. France has not gone to war. The Czechs were stupid and foolish to mobilize. . . ."

"And now," Von Ribbentrop replied bitterly, "Germans in the Sudetenland are being murdered in cold blood."

"It is better to lose a few lives than for millions to perish," Henderson said.

"A solution better be reached very shortly," the Nazi foreign minister warned, "or all Germany will rise as one. . . ."

Georges Bonnet, in Paris, was frantic when informed that the Czechoslovaks had mobilized without consulting France and Great Britain. Surely, the next step was mobilization by the Germans, which would bring on that of France. It looked to Bonnet as though war were inevitable.

"Paris will be destroyed by the German bombers. Oh, those accursed Czechs! Those stiff-necked idiots!" the French foreign minister cried to an aide.

Regaining his composure, however, he called in newspaper correspondents on the evening of May 21 and announced that if the Germans violated Czechoslovakia's borders, "France will stand by her treaty with the Czechs. . . . I hope and pray," he added, "that Germany will do nothing to put France in a position where her treaty obligations will oblige her to intervene. . . ."

Privately, Bonnet informed German embassy officials that his statement was "eyewash" and "window dressing." The French government had no intention of "upsetting the applecart" by making any aggressive moves against Germany. "That is," Bonnet cautioned, "if you Germans don't lose your heads and attack us."

Britain's foreign minister, Lord Halifax, informed the French government that Britain would come to the aid of France only if she were the victim of unprovoked aggression by Germany. The French must not assume that His Majesty's government would undertake joint military action to defend Czechoslovakia from the Germans. Halifax also "warned" the German Foreign Office that Britain would take "appropriate measures" if Germany invaded France. As for the Czechoslovaks, Halifax promised that Great

Britain would continue to urge Prague to reach a peaceful settlement with Germany.

Halifax's statement pleased Bonnet, who hastened to advise London that France, too, would press the Prague government to satisfy German demands on the Sudeten issue. If the Czechoslovaks proved unreasonable, Bonnet said, France would consider herself released from the alliance.

"We will do nothing to provoke the Germans," he promised. "We will make no move without first consulting the British government and receiving its consent. . . ."

Throughout the period of May 20–21, during which the German attack had been expected, Czechoslovak anti-aircraft gunners anxiously watched the skies for the anticipated swarms of Luftwaffe bombers. Planes and pilots of the small but excellent Czechoslovak Air Force were ready to respond at a moment's notice when needed.

In the bunkers and forts of the "Little Maginot Line" that guarded the nation's borders, tense soldiers stood at firing ports. Artillery batteries zeroed in on potential targets. Machine-gun nests were manned. Sentries scanned roads for *panzers* (tanks) and Nazi shock troops.

None came.

No bombs fell on Prague. No *panzers* rolled. Guns remained silent.

The war scare had been a false alarm.

For once, the Nazis had been telling the truth. They had concentrated no forces to assault the Czechoslovaks. The movements by Wehrmacht, Luftwaffe, and other military units had been in preparation for annual spring maneuvers.

The Nazis were not yet fully prepared to invade Czechoslovakia. Hitler still fussed with details of Case Green and was withholding approval of the plan until it met his complete satisfaction.

The swiftness of the Czechoslovak move startled him, but had Case Green been polished, the mobilization would not have forestalled a scheduled invasion. The Czechoslovak Army as such did not worry Hitler. What did concern him, however, was the strength of the Czechoslovak fortifications—the great steel and concrete forts, bunkers, and blockhouses which might well slow down the Wehrmacht for all its armored might. His shock troops, especially trained to attack fortified positions, needed more practice before the Fuehrer would send them into combat.

On Monday, May 23, Hitler ordered Foreign Minister von Ribbentrop to tell Vojtech Mastny, the Czechoslovak envoy in Berlin, that Germany had no aggressive intentions toward Czechoslovakia, and that all reports of German troop concentrations were untrue.

A sigh of relief went up from London, Paris, Prague, and Moscow. The May Crisis was over. British, French, Czechoslovak, and Russian leaders felt that at last Hitler had been taught a lesson.

The success of the mobilization filled the Czechoslovaks with confidence. The Prague government was perfectly willing to talk about the Sudetenland; but if Henlein's demands were not eased, they were prepared to throw him in jail on treason charges.

As for the Fuehrer, the May Crisis only strengthened his determination to destroy Czechoslovakia. After stewing and fuming at his mountain retreat near Berchtesgaden for a few days, Hitler went to Berlin and called a meeting of his top military leaders to discuss the changes he had made in Case Green.

Actually, the plan was only slightly modified. But there was one major change. Hitler now declared: *"It is my unalterable decision to smash Czechoslovakia by military action in the near future. . . ."* The "near future," Hitler revealed, was October 1, 1938. "Case Green must be executed on that date, come what may. I will wait no longer. My patience is ended. The patience of the German people is ended. The Sudeten question will be settled once and for all—my way!" Hitler thundered at his generals.

That date, October 1, was one which Hitler would hold to unshakably through the long, crisis-ridden summer.

CHAPTER 9

The May Crisis, which had repercussions all over Europe, caused little anxiety among ordinary French citizens. Throughout the turbulent forty-eight hours of May 21–22, the people of France behaved as though nothing untoward was happening. Taking advantage of the pleasant spring weather, families went picnicking in the country; lovers strolled along the Seine; idlers sipped Pernod and cognac at boulevard cafes in Paris.

Only in the industrial districts and the so-called "Red Belt"—the working-class sections—of Paris was there any apparent reaction to the crisis. In these areas Communists and other left-wingers organized demonstrations calling on the government to support the Czechoslovaks. Nazi sympathizers called counterdemonstrations, and a few bloody free-for-alls erupted. Gendarmes, swinging clubs and lead-weighted capes, soon separated the brawlers.

There was no extraordinary military movement in France. No leaves were canceled, no reserves called to the colors. The Ministry of War announced, however, that the French Army was in readiness for any circumstances; this was the great advantage of the Maginot Line, a ranking general pointed out—the fortifications did not require large numbers of troops; the usual peacetime garrisons were sufficient.

If the French public remained calm, the same could not be said of the Foreign Office, where a condition verging on hysteria prevailed. Georges Bonnet dashed from one embassy to another, reminding one American observer of "a stray dog with firecrackers tied to his tail. . . ."

During a call on Johannes Welsczeck, the German ambassador, Bonnet frantically pleaded for "restraint" by the Nazis. He promised that France would work to win "70 percent of the Sudetenlanders' demands."

Publicly, Bonnet displayed a different image. The people thought he was defying the Nazis, when all the while he was "carrying the ball for Hitler," in the words of an American newsman.

The May Crisis brought home to the average Englishman the very real danger of war, but most Britons accepted the fact calmly. In London pubs men sipped ale and talked about "giving old Hitler a knocking about." Few seemed concerned that the British Army was undersized and underequipped or that the Royal Air Force had so few planes.

As in France, the government lacked the courage of the people. At the height of the crisis, Chamberlain called a cabinet meeting. It was agreed that war must be avoided, even though the price would be high. "Any appeasement of Hitler is better than a holocaust," one cabinet official said.

The Chamberlain cabinet was more upset by the Czechoslovak mobilization than by the suspected Nazi threat that had caused it. When the immediate danger of war passed, Chamberlain and his colleagues resolved that another such crisis must be prevented; the next time, Hitler might decide to march. According to Chamberlain, the only way to avert a repetition of the May Crisis was for the Czechoslovaks to come to terms which satisfied Henlein and Hitler. Bonnet and, to a lesser extent, Daladier, agreed with the British on this question. From now on, the main efforts of the two governments would be directed to that end.

The May Crisis also had its effect in the United States. Despite involvement in their own economic troubles, Americans closely followed the events of that tense weekend on the radio. Pro-Nazis tried to drum up support for Hitler, but anti-Nazi demonstrations outnumbered and drowned out the homegrown Fascists.

Secretary of State Cordell Hull spoke to the ambassadors of Germany, France, and Czechoslovakia, urging them to work for peace. President Roosevelt sent personal messages to the heads of those countries asking them to shun war as a means of "solving international difficulties."

For most Americans, however, the occurrences of May 21–22 were remote; at the time, a spirit of isolationism influenced public and private thinking. "Let's keep our noses out of Europe," the isolationists said. Much of the country agreed. There were, of course, dissenters who demanded that the United States help "quarantine the aggressor" and called for "collective security," a policy that would bring all democratic nations into a solid front against the Nazis and Fascists. But they were in a minority.

Americans looked forward to the upcoming Memorial Day holiday for which a long-range weather forecaster predicted unclouded skies and temperatures in the high seventies. It would be a day for the beach, a picnic, or the traditional doubleheader at the local ballpark.

War was for Europeans.

"Thank God You're an American!" crowed William Randolph Hearst's New York *Journal-American* in a front-page editorial. "Amen!" echoed the paper's readers.

Across the Atlantic, diplomats and politicians evaluated the May Crisis. Czechoslovakia's defiant action had achieved some positive results. Although embittered because their region had been occupied by the Czechoslovak Army, the Sudetenlanders limited themselves to glowering and grumbling. The presence of Czechoslovak troops abruptly ended the disorders that had been bringing anarchy to the Sudetenland.

The area was sufficiently calm so that local elections were held as scheduled on May 22, May 29, and June 12. They went off entirely without incident; more smoothly, in fact, than they had for several years. "The bayonets of Prague's soldiers were a soothing influence," an observer stated. "They cooled the ardor of even the most fervent Sudeten Nazi."

The outcome of the elections was predictable. In the Sudeten region, Henlein's Sudeten German Party swamped the anti-Nazi parties, receiving 91.4 percent of the vote. In the non-German sectors of the country, Eduard Benes' National Social Party and Prime Minister Milan Hodza's Agrarian Party won an overwhelming vote of confidence. In contradiction to Nazi propaganda that the "Reds" would win the election, the Communists and Socialists lost much ground.

69

Despite his sweeping victory, Konrad Henlein declared, "We Sudeten Germans are living under the gun in a military dictatorship. While the boots of Prague's soldiers trample our liberties, we will not meet with leaders of the Czech government nor will we negotiate with tyrants. We demand the removal of the army so we may breathe as free men, not a conquered people."

This outcry for demobilization of the Czechoslovak Army was vehemently echoed in Berlin. London and Paris raised the same demand. Prague's allies applied constant pressure on President Benes, arguing that a mobilized Czechoslovak Army presented a "threat" to peace.

Benes refused to be hurried into demobilization, however. If the elections passed without trouble, he promised, some units would be released after June 12. This was not good enough for London; again and again, one British official or another pressed the Czechoslovak government.

"Demobilize! Demobilize! That's all they keep repeating. One might think we're responsible for all the trouble and not Henlein or Hitler; that we, not the Nazis, are turning Europe inside out!" a Czechoslovak cabinet member complained.

At last, on May 29, the Czechoslovaks started releasing some troops. During the first days of June, fifty thousand men were sent home, and Prague promised not to call up reservists after June 12, except for annual training. By the end of June, all reserves were out of uniform; but the Regular Army remained on a limited alert basis.

Ironically, the Czechoslovak show of strength worsened rather than bettered the country's position. The independence of the Prague government convinced men such as Chamberlain, Halifax, and Bonnet that the Benes regime must be weakened to prevent another "May Crisis," which might lead to war. The British and French appeasers made it clear that if Czechoslovakia ever again took such action without their permission, the little country would be left to its fate.

"We shall regard any military steps by the Czechs as a provocation for war. . . . In that event we will have not even a moral obligation towards her," a British spokesman said.

"He means that we should behave like sheep being led to

slaughter," a Czechoslovak journalist remarked. "But after the Nazi ax has fallen, those fine gentlemen in Whitehall and the Quai d'Orsay will shed bitter tears at our funeral. . . . With such friends, we have more than our share of enemies. . . ."

1. Wilhelm I, the German Kaiser, resplendent in full-dress uniform, salutes as he sets out to inspect troops at a military review shortly before the outbreak of World War I. Accompanying the Kaiser are bemedaled officers of the Imperial General Staff. (WIDE WORLD)

2. Revolutionary German soldiers and civilians aboard a truck flying the red flag pose for photographers on a Berlin street during anti-monarchist uprisings in November 1918, prior to Wilhelm's abdication. (UPI)

3. Atop a horse-drawn ambulance parked before Berlin's Imperial Palace, an agitator exhorts a crowd on January 3, 1919, as Reds seek to incite full-scale revolution, and to establish a Russian-style government in defeated Germany. (UPI)

4. BELOW RIGHT. In 1923, Germany's economic collapse brought on inflation so devastating that money was almost worthless. This Berlin theater has a sign over the box office announcing a barter system for admission tickets. The cheapest seats cost two eggs, the best ones go for a pound of butter apiece. (ADN/ZENTRALBILD)

5. Socialist leader Friedrich Ebert, once a saddle-maker, is snapped with his wife while strolling on a snowy Berlin street in February 1919, just after becoming the first President of the German Republic. (WIDE WORLD)

6. Seventy-eight years old in April 1925, Field Marshal Paul von Hindenburg, Germany's most revered war hero, doffs his high hat before Berlin spectators, on the way to his inauguration as the Republic's second President. The aged soldier was elected to office following Ebert's death earlier that year. (WIDE WORLD)

7. BELOW LEFT. Czechoslovakia's founder and first President, Tomas Garrigue Masaryk (1850–1937), sits for a photograph in 1934. Leader of the nation since 1918, Masaryk retired in 1935, and was succeeded by Dr. Eduard Benes. (WIDE WORLD)

8. Dr. Eduard Benes RIGHT, second President of the Czech Republic, talks with Milan Hodza, the country's premier, at an outdoor reception in Prague, in July 1938, when the Sudeten crisis was boiling. Born in 1884, Dr. Benes died in 1948, having seen Czechoslovakia liberated from the Germans, then lost to Soviet-supported Czech Communists. (WIDE WORLD)

9. Konrad Henlein, once a gym master, is seen in a reflective mood. Leader of the Sudeten Nazis, Henlein helped bring on the downfall of the Prague government by opening the way for Nazi occupation of the country after the Munich Pact. Captured by Americans in 1945, Henlein committed suicide rather than stand trial for treason. (USIA)

10. On October 4, 1938, four days after the Munich Pact signing, Henlein addresses a Nazi rally at Asch, Czechoslovakia. Raptly listening from his place on the platform is Adolf Hitler, the German Fuehrer, flanked by German and Czech Nazi dignitaries. (WIDE WORLD)

11. Enthusiastically greeted by residents giving the Nazi salute, singing, rifle-toting Sudeten Nazis, jauntily wearing flowers in their lapels, march into a Czech border village near Henlein's home town, Asch. (WIDE WORLD)

12. Czech Ambassador to Great Britain, Jan Masaryk (1886–1948), Tomas Masaryk's son, walks along a London street after a fruitless talk with British Foreign Minister Lord Halifax, August 31, 1938. During the 1948 Prague Communist coup, Masaryk died under mysterious circumstances. Officially, he was reported to have taken his own life, but reliable sources believe the Reds murdered him. (USIA)

13. Traveling by airplane for the first time in his life, Prime Minister Neville Chamberlain flew to Berchtesgaden, Germany, on September 15, 1938, to discuss the Czech crisis with Hitler. The meeting was held at the Berghof, the Fuehrer's mountain retreat, shown here. (ADN/ZENTRALBILD)

14. Conference participants pause for tea in the lavishly appointed Berghof salon. Facing camera (l. to r.): Nazi Foreign Minister Joachim von Ribbentrop; Prime Minister Neville Chamberlain; Adolf Hitler; interpreter Paul Schmidt, and Sir Neville Henderson, Britain's Ambassador to Germany. (UPI)

15. Picturesque Godesberg, a resort city on the Rhine River, was chosen as the site for the second round of talks between the British and the Germans. The meetings, held September 22–23, 1938, accomplished little. World tensions remained at a fever pitch, and war over the Czech situation seemed unavoidable. (USIA)

16. The sumptuous Hotel Petersberg, perched atop a hill overlooking the Rhine, served as headquarters for the British delegation during the Godesberg talks, which took place on the Rhine's left bank in the equally elegant Hotel Dreesen. (USIA)

17. British Union Jack and Nazi swastika flags lend a mildly festive air to the exterior of the venerable Hotel Dreesen, the day before the conference opened. Placid townspeople look on as Godesberg awaits the arrival of the delegations. (WIDE WORLD)

CHAPTER 10

As spring became summer, Dr. Goebbels kept the "Hate Czechoslovakia" campaign going full blast. Hardly a day went by that the Nazi press did not headline some new Czechoslovak "atrocity" in the Sudetenland. Naturally, Prague resented such attacks, and a countercampaign of anti-German propaganda flowed over Czechoslovak airwaves and appeared in the newspapers.

The Sudeten question remained unsolved, although there was no lack of proposed solutions. Henlein, at Hitler's behest, presented to Prague several unacceptable blueprints to end the Sudetenland's troubles. Henlein's plans were all rejected because the acceptance of even the mildest of them meant the dissolution of the Czechoslovak Republic.

In turn, Benes offered at least two bills which would have provided the national minorities in Czechoslovakia the fairest treatment of any country with a minority problem. Among other concessions, government jobs, public services, and schools would be granted to minorities in proportion to their numbers.

The minorities would have autonomous control over the schools. Minority languages would be declared an official tongue in certain regions, even where less than 20 percent of the population used them. All governmental employees would be required to have a knowledge of minority languages.

These farsighted proposals were hailed as an emancipation proclamation by most Czechoslovak minorities. But the Sudetenlanders turned them down, demanding full equality with the Prague government. Henlein later confided to an aide, "Benes tempted me sorely. Had we accepted his bills, they would have provided a basis for full agreement with the Czechs. But I knew the Fuehrer did not want such a settlement."

Discussion of the minority bills ended when another storm broke over the Sudetenland. On July 17, reports and rumors circulated in Prague that heavy German troop movements were taking place in Austria. At the same time, Berlin announced that the Czechoslovaks had mobilized again. According to the Nazis, Prague's troops were "swarming up to the frontier," and "spreading terror throughout the Sudetenland."

Prime Minister Chamberlain telephoned Henderson in Berlin and asked him for accurate facts on these disturbing reports. Henderson assured Chamberlain that British observers in various parts of the Reich had seen nothing unusual going on. London was also reassured by Sir Basil Newton from Prague that no Czechoslovak mobilization had occurred.

The scare had been manufactured—possibly by Joseph Goebbels.

When this brief flurry of excitement died down, Sir Neville Henderson, in a highly unusual outburst of emotion, said to a secretary, "How much longer must we continue to suffer the torment of these crises? The time has come to stop them! We must let Prague have a real twist of the screw!"

At the height of the July Crisis, there appeared in London one Captain Fritz Wiedemann, who had been Hitler's company commander during the 1914–18 war. Wiedemann was in the British capital to deliver for his Fuehrer a personal message to Lord Halifax, the burden of which was that Hitler could not be moved by threats or by force. The Fuehrer wanted Halifax to know that "the Sudeten question must and shall be settled. . . ." It made little difference to Hitler whether this was accomplished by peace or by war.

During his conversation with Wiedemann, the British foreign minister asked the captain for a declaration that Germany had no intention of invading Czechoslovakia or of using force against that country in any way.

"That depends on Benes," Captain Wiedemann said. "Not for a moment does the Fuehrer wish to harm a neighbor. However, if incidents continue in the Sudetenland, Germany will not remain passive."

74

This was scarcely the sort of pledge to allay fears of a Nazi attack on the Czechoslovaks, but it satisfied Halifax. In a cordial parting with Wiedemann, the foreign minister said, "My fondest wish, before I die, the culmination of my life's work, would be to see the Fuehrer entering Buckingham Palace at the side of King George, amidst the acclamations of the English people. . . ."

(The vision of rapport between England and Nazi Germany had not originated with Halifax. It was the goal of a group of high-ranking Britons, known as the Cliveden Set, which included noblemen and wealthy commoners. According to rumors then current, the Duke of Windsor, the former King Edward VIII, who had abdicated the throne in 1936 to marry Wallis Simpson, an American, also belonged to the Cliveden Set.)

Despite Wiedemann's assurance that Germany sought to preserve peace, the Nazis continued, during the remainder of July and throughout August, to provoke the Czechoslovaks. Such important Nazi leaders as Rudolf Hess, the third deputy Fuehrer, threatened the Czechoslovaks with extinction unless they ceased "persecuting the Sudetenlanders." Inflammatory speeches against Czechoslovakia were delivered by Goebbels, Von Ribbentrop, Goering, and Hitler himself.

In the face of all this, Benes counseled patience and calmness. "Let the Nazis rant and rave; let them revile us with undeserved insults and accusations. We know the truth and shall not fall into Hitler's clumsy trap. In our dealings with the Sudeten people, we shall continue to display fairness and firmness. If war comes, no shred of guilt will be ours; as in the past, the onus of guilt will be on the Germans," the Czechoslovak President said.

Perhaps the most ardent anti-Prague demonstration took place at Breslau, in German Silesia, near the Czechoslovak border. On July 25, a huge gymnastic festival was held there. Among the honored guests was Konrad Henlein, who addressed the huge crowd. "We Sudetenlanders," he declared, "are Germans, first, last, and always, part and parcel of the Third Reich. We are one folk, one Reich, with one leader!"

The highlight of the festival was a mammoth parade on July 31, in which thousands of gymnasts participated. Hitler was in the reviewing stand, and as the Sudetenland contingent swung past, the marchers suddenly broke ranks and rushed up to him. Weep-

75

ing women and girls tossed flowers at his feet. "Beloved Fuehrer," they screamed. "Help us! Help us! Take us home to the Fatherland!"

In a voice that echoed over the public address system loudspeakers, Hitler cried, "My faithful Sudetenlanders! I have not forsaken you! Your Fuehrer promises that you will not be forgotten! One day, soon, you shall again belong to the Fatherland! I swear this on my life!"

Pandemonium broke out among the Sudeten marchers. They cheered, wept, and screamed. In unison more than thirty thousand voices chanted, *"Heil* Hitler! *Seig heil!"* A Swedish newspaperman, covering the Breslau gymnastic festival, wrote: "The shouts of adulation rose and fell like mountainous waves breaking on a rocky shore. . . . It was hard to believe that such thunderous noise was emitted by human throats. . . . To the Sudetenlanders, to all Germans, Adolf Hitler is not a political figure—he is a divinity, a Teutonic god come to life. . . ."

Even before the fervent outburst at Breslau, the fragile balance of peace had become more precarious. French military intelligence reports revealed that the Germans were working full tilt at building a fortified line along their western frontier.

Known as the Westwall, or Siegfried Line, it was not as grandiose as the Maginot Line, but it was formidable enough, with its steel and concrete bunkers, deep trenches, rows of antitank obstacles called "Dragon's Teeth," and numerous machine-gun emplacements. According to French information, the Westwall was scheduled for completion on August 15.

This was a cause of grave concern to France and Britain. Just as disturbing was news that the Germans were stockpiling stores of oil and gas for the Luftwaffe. At the same time, Air Force reservists had been called for active duty. All leaves in the Luftwaffe and the Wehrmacht were canceled, and additional classes of men were being drafted. Officials in London and Paris feared that these moves were steps preparatory to a Nazi attack on Czechoslovakia in the fall.

Sir Neville Henderson notified Chamberlain that Berlin was getting increasingly impatient about the Sudeten situation. Any minor incident in the Sudetenland was liable "to light the fuse," he warned.

76

Henderson also advised London that the Germans felt that the Czechoslovaks were stalling in negotiations over the Sudetenland. "We must do something drastic, else it will be impossible to prevent war. Herr Hitler will not wait much longer," Sir Neville wrote to the Prime Minister.

Since the accepted ways of settling the Sudeten Crisis appeared to have failed, Chamberlain and Halifax decided that a British mediator, empowered to deal with the Sudetenlanders and the Czechoslovaks, should be sent to Prague. According to the initial plan, the mediator would hear the arguments of both sides and then evolve a compromise settlement. Neither Paris nor Prague were consulted in this decision.

The idea of a "neutral" mediator had long been brewing in the minds of both Chamberlain and Halifax. The man selected for the delicate mission was Walter Runciman, a millionaire banking, shipping, and railroad tycoon. The sixty-eight-year-old businessman had served as a Member of Parliament since 1899, and had entered the House of Lords in 1937, with the title First Viscount Runciman.

A journalist wrote that Runciman "seemed to have fallen from a page of Dickens and resented his fall. . . ." Characterized as possessing a mind "crammed with facts . . . a veritable human balance sheet," Runciman had a great passion for German classical music. He spoke fluent German, but no Czechoslovak, and had often expressed his admiration for Hitler.

A Danish reporter said of Runciman, "He is no more neutral about the Sudeten issue than a housebreaker trying to decide whether to steal jewelry or cash. . . ."

The news that Runciman had agreed to undertake the assignment was given the French by Lord Halifax on July 20, during a state visit to France of King George VI and Queen Elizabeth. Premier Daladier and Foreign Minister Bonnet were delighted. Working jointly with Chamberlain and Halifax, they pressured the Czechoslovaks to accept the Runciman mission.

President Benes resented what he considered an affront to Czechoslovakia's sovereignty. If the British and French wanted to sponsor a mediator, the least they could have done was to let the Czechoslovak government know their intentions. Benes set aside his objections, however, and on July 23 officially requested outside help to overcome the Sudeten "difficulties."

No matter what lofty motives Chamberlain ascribed to the Runciman mission, the mediator was in fact a British agent. His task was not to ensure a just resolution of the situation, but to force the Czechoslovaks to accept a solution which appeased the Sudeten Nazis.

A left-wing British political observer said of the Runciman mission: "The so-called mediator is a soft soap artist come to sell the Czechs a bill of goods which they had better buy, like it or not. . . ."

Once Benes had agreed to the mission, the British government sought Berlin's approval. For political reasons, however, Hitler refused to accept Runciman, although he advised Henlein to do so.

The Runciman mission arrived in Prague on August 3, 1938. Its coming marked a shift in the handling of the Sudetenland question; no longer would Czechoslovakia conduct negotiations as an independent and sovereign state. Foreigners, under the direction of a foreign government, had taken the direction of policy away from the Czechoslovaks.

The road that led to the Munich Pact was now open; by agreeing to accept Runciman, the Czechoslovaks had surrendered their independence of action. It was to prove a tragic mistake.

CHAPTER 11

Neville Chamberlain had personally chosen Walter Runciman to conduct the mission to Czechoslovakia. Of his choice he said, "We are fortunate to have obtained Viscount Runciman's services. . . . He has outstanding personal qualifications for the task; experience in dealing with men of all sorts under all conditions. . . . Personally, he is fearless, free from prejudice; a man of integrity and impartiality. . . ."

This paragon was accompanied to Prague by his wife and several associates, among them Frank T. A. Ashton-Gwatkin, who headed the economic section of the Foreign Office; R. J. Stopford, an expert on India and international finance; Geoffrey Peto, Runciman's parliamentary private secretary; and a member of the consular service named Ian Henderson (no relation to Sir Neville).

Soon after his arrival, Runciman held a press conference in the main ballroom of Prague's Alcron Hotel, where the mission was staying. He told the assembled newsmen, "In forty years of political experience, I have learned that peace and tranquility can only be established on the basis of mutual consent. . . . I am a friend to all, an enemy to none. . . ."

The Runciman mission made a deep impression on the people of Prague; not for anything they said or did, but because each of these proper Englishmen wore a morning coat, striped trousers, and a top hat in the sweltering midsummer heat.

Although Runciman and his associates looked like diplomats, they were hardly prepared for the role. Runciman's experience in

79

negotiations had been confined to labor disputes and trade union contracts; he had no firsthand knowledge of international affairs. Neither had the improbably named Ashton-Gwatkin or the Indian expert, R. J. Stopford. The Runciman mission was almost totally unqualified to perform its stated purpose; not one of its members was an authority on central European affairs or the complications of national minorities.

The Czechoslovak government cooperated with Runciman, but a wide gap existed between the mediator and the Prague cabinet. Conversations had to be carried out through a translator; Benes spoke French, but no English or German. Although fairly fluent in German, Runciman knew neither French nor Czechoslovak. His dealings with the President were complicated and unsatisfactory.

Runciman came away from one such conference saying, "I do not believe President Benes has much understanding or respect for the Germans in Czechoslovakia. . . . For some reason he believes that autonomy in the Sudetenland would destroy the Czechoslovak state. . . ."

Day after day, Runciman presided over sessions between Sudeten representatives and Czechoslovak government officials. The negotiations led nowhere; neither side would yield an inch. After a while, the mediator's pro-Sudeten bias began to show. Sudeten leaders spoke German, and he could deal with them directly. Realizing their advantage, the Sudeten Nazis made an open play for Runciman's sympathy. At every opportunity, they recited tales of persecution at the hands of the Czechoslovaks.

On instructions from Berlin, the Sudeten leaders campaigned to make Runciman believe the Czechoslovak government would never grant them concessions. They placed the blame for the disturbed state of Europe on the Czechoslovaks alone. Gradually, Runciman and his colleagues began to accept this lopsided view of the situation.

The weekend of August 15, Runciman was a guest at the estate of Ulrich Krinsky, a wealthy Sudetenlander, and a member of Henlein's party. Krinsky took the mediator on a tour of the district, pointing out what he claimed were Sudeten-owned businesses driven into bankruptcy by the Czechoslovaks.

This impressed businessman Runciman; but even more impressive was a "spontaneous" demonstration of "suffering" Sudeten women and children at the gates of Krinsky's estate.

When the crowd spotted Runciman sitting beside his host in the latter's limousine, they cried, "Help us, please, Lord Runciman! Save us! Save us!"

On his return from the Krinsky estate, Runciman upbraided an astonished Benes for permitting "untrammeled persecution" of the Sudetenlanders. Runciman then asked the Sudeten negotiators for a man-to-man talk with Henlein, whom he had not yet met. This request was granted. The Sudeten Fuehrer and his staff met Runciman and his aides at a castle in the Sudetenland.

Henlein spoke simply and to the point. He had no desire to break up the Czechoslovak state; all he wanted was autonomy for his people and freedom from persecution. "I am an advocate of peace; I hate war and violence," he assured Runciman. Henlein further declared that he had no sympathy with Nazi terror and promised to protect "our Jewish brethren" from "anti-Semitic fanatics."

After the meeting, Mr. Ashton-Gwatkin sent a favorable report on Henlein to Prime Minister Chamberlain. "He is, I am sure, an absolutely honest fellow . . . especially in his feelings about future relations between Germany and England after the Czech-Sudeten business is settled. . . . Henlein wants Anglo-German amity. . . . I believe he means this; and I believe he will help us achieve a splendid relationship with Hitler. . . ."

The Czechoslovak position was further undermined by Chamberlain's foreign policy adviser, Sir Horace Wilson, who told a German Embassy official that the British government regarded Czechoslovakia as "an air cushion out of which the air is gradually escaping." According to Wilson, His Majesty's government would do anything, meet any terms, to satisfy the Germans.

"Only the Bolsheviks will benefit from an Anglo-German war," Wilson said. Once a settlement of the Sudeten question was obtained, Britain would not object to German domination of southeastern Europe. "All we ask is that you do not shut us out of the trading there; leave us only 20 percent."

Although speaking off the record, Sir Horace reflected the official views of the British government. Wilson even went so far as to say, "Nothing will deter the Prime Minister from reaching an understanding with Germany. . . . We will do all possible to make the Czechs come around. . . ."

How much farther "around" President Benes could possibly come remained undefined. On August 24, the harassed Czechoslovak leader gave in to almost all of Henlein's Karlsbad demands, only to be turned down because some of the Sudeten requirements had not been met.

"My God!" Benes exclaimed at this rejection. "What will satisfy them? Must I tear Czechoslovakia to pieces?"

Ashton-Gwatkin and Runciman listened coldly to the President's complaints. "You must do what is necessary," Runciman said. "If you grant the Karlsbad demands, plus a few reasonable additional concessions, I can go home and consider the job well done."

"But my country!" Benes cried. "I cannot play fast and loose with my country's future. Do you think Hitler will be content even if we give Henlein all he asks and more? The Nazi will not stop until he has swallowed Czechoslovakia!"

Runciman refused to listen to such talk. Upon leaving Benes, he confided to an aide, "In my opinion, the Czech won't be happy unless it comes to a war. He thinks we and the French will pull his chestnuts out of the fire. Well, that's not highly likely. Not likely at all!"

While the Runciman mission pursued its ineffectual negotiations and London prepared to sell out Czechoslovakia, French leaders, especially Bonnet, continued bowing and scraping before the Germans. Georges Bonnet claimed, in a private talk with Johannes Welsczeck, the German ambassador, that most of the French people, perhaps "90 percent," wished for an understanding with Germany.

Both he and Daladier, Bonnet assured Welsczeck, admired Hitler. "Without bloodshed, the Fuehrer has made possible the grandiose reconstruction of Germany and carried it out in a fashion which no one would have believed possible before the 1914–18 war," Bonnet said admiringly.

To cap his magnificent achievements, Hitler must attain a

peaceful revision of the Versailles Treaty and reach an understanding with Great Britain and France, Bonnet continued. Having accomplished this, the Fuehrer would well deserve acclamation as "this century's greatest statesman."

Bonnet promised the German ambassador that France would force Prague to yield to the Sudetens; in fact, the French foreign minister declared, the Sudetenland should be incorporated into the German Reich. Personally, Bonnet confided, he would do all in his power to make sure that this happened.

As he had before, the ambitious politician strode both sides of the controversy. In a speech made only two days after his chat with Welsczeck, Bonnet told an audience of metalworkers: "France will remain faithful to her pacts. No matter what others may do, we shall not let down those who depend upon us!"

All through August, the fruitless bickering over the Sudetenland continued. No matter how much Benes conceded, Henlein rejected his proposals. The Sudeten Nazi faithfully obeyed Hitler's instructions to keep negotiating, keep stalling, keep refusing. The Fuehrer was readying the ultimate solution of the Sudeten problem.

Day by day, the preparations for Case Green were being carried out: more troops were trained, more weapons, planes, and military stores manufactured. By October 1, the German high command assured Hitler, the Wehrmacht and the Luftwaffe would be ready for any task the Fuehrer demanded.

The British and French leaders seemed more concerned about Czechoslovak "stubbornness" in the Sudeten negotiations than the overt Nazi military buildup. Chamberlain and his ministers acted as though President Benes was the only stumbling block to peace.

On August 31, Lord Halifax sent Runciman a note urging him to "twist the Czech President's tail." Any solution the Runciman mission proposed must be accepted by Benes, or else "the Czechs will have to look after themselves."

Runciman called upon Benes the next day and told him that the mission recommended nothing less than the Karlsbad demands; only this would be agreeable to Henlein. If Benes remained adamant, the mediator warned, Czechoslovakia would be left on its own to face either German intervention or civil war.

"For our part, Czechoslovakia can sink or swim," Runciman declared. "We simply do not care. If Britain has to choose between your acceptance of the Karlsbad demands and war, do not remain under any illusions as to what our choice will be."

Similar warnings were delivered to Beñes by the French ambassador. And President Roosevelt shattered any hope the Czechoslovak President might have harbored about support from the United States.

Referring to a speech made by William C. Bullitt, U. S. ambassador to France, in which he had said: ". . . if war breaks out in Europe, no one can state or foretell whether or not the United States would be drawn into such a war . . . ," FDR clarified the American position: "To include the United States in a Franco-British front against Hitler, is . . . 100 percent wrong. . . . Ambassador Bullitt's speech does not constitute . . . a moral engagement on the part of the United States towards the democracies. . . ."

As if this were not enough, the London *Times,* frequently a mouthpiece of the British government, ran an editorial which read in part:

"If the Sudetens now ask for more than the Czechoslovak government are ready to give in their latest set of proposals. . . . it might be worthwhile for the Czechoslovak government to consider whether they should exclude altogether the project . . . of making Czechoslovakia a more homogenous state by the cession of that fringe of alien populations who are contiguous to the nation to which they are united by race. . . ."

In plain language, the London *Times* was suggesting the breakup of the Czechoslovak Republic by ceding areas with national minorities to their "homelands": Hungarian Czechoslovaks to Hungary, Rumanians to Rumania, Poles to Poland, Germans to Germany. "In that case," a Czechoslovak newspaperman wrote, "What would we have left? Why did not the venerable *Times* come out in favor of restoring the Austro-Hungarian Empire?"

Pressed from all sides, President Benes could hold out no longer. Even he could now see that the independence of Czechoslovakia, which France and Britain had so solemnly pledged in 1918, was not worth the paper on which that pledge had been written.

Benes prepared to yield. If appeasement was the spirit of the times then he had to become an appeaser.

CHAPTER 12

On Sunday, September 4, President Benes summoned to the presidential palace two Sudeten German representatives, Ernst Kundt and Wilhelm Sebekovsky.

The President astounded the two men by bluntly stating, "Write down your demands and I will grant them at once." When Kundt and Sebekovsky hesitated, Benes said, "Very well, then. Perhaps it will be more appropriate if you dictate them to me."

Uncapping his fountain pen, he wrote as the Sudetens listed their demands. When they were finished, the President signed the paper. "I promise to grant everything you have asked. Tell that to Henlein. You have won, gentlemen! The corpse of Czechoslovakia is your prize!"

A cabinet meeting at which each Sudeten demand was considered, convened on Monday, September 5. The result was a proposal known as the Fourth Plan, which came within a hair of meeting Henlein's Karlsbad program. Under the Fourth Plan every minority group was granted virtual autonomy.

Each district would be governed by its predominant nationality. All bureaus of the federal government would have minority sections. The German, Russian, Magyar, Polish, and Czechoslovak languages were to be official. The Czechoslovak budget would be apportioned among the various minorities.

On only two points did the Fourth Plan fail to meet Henlein's demands. The Sudetenland was not to be a legal entity but part of the Czechoslovak state, and the Nazi ideology was not accepted as the ruling philosophy for the region.

Benes could go no farther if Czechoslovakia were to survive as a nation. Possibly, the Fourth Plan went too far; had it been adopted, every central government document would have had to be translated into five languages; this alone might have rendered Prague impotent and brought on the dissolution of the nation.

The Fourth Plan had been drawn up not to satisfy the Sudetenlanders, but rather to mollify Great Britain and France, for President Benes still feared complete isolation from the west. Speaking of the plan, Benes told Runciman and Sir Basil Newton, the British ambassador, "This is total capitulation; in the near future, Great Britain and France will regret forcing us to take such a drastic step. . . ."

Neither Newton nor Runciman were moved. Nor did politicians in London and Paris pay any attention to the Czechoslovak President's prophetic warning. The Fourth Plan was a godsend to the appeasers. It seemed to settle all Sudeten grievances except for the two minor considerations which certainly could be ironed out.

Even the Sudeten leaders did not see how they could reject the plan. It represented almost complete victory for them. After having played the role of martyrs for so long, they were confused by their unexpected triumph.

The Fourth Plan posed a serious problem for Hitler and Henlein, since it removed their carefully prepared rationale for the destruction of the Czechoslovak state. As Ernst Kundt pointed out, unless the Fourth Plan were accepted, the whole world would realize that the Sudetenlanders, not the Czechoslovaks, had been responsible for all the past trouble. Their participation in Hitler's plot to seize Czechoslovakia for the Third Reich would be exposed.

The Sudeten Nazis were rescued from this dilemma, however, by an incident that occurred at Mährisch-Ostrau, a Sudeten town, which happened to have a more than 80 percent Czechoslovak population.

On Wednesday, September 7, deputies of the Sudeten German Party visited some local Nazis imprisoned on charges of gun running. The schoolmaster, a German, decided that the occasion was important enough to dismiss classes for the day. The town's Nazis turned out to greet the deputies at the jailhouse. Before long several hundred German men, women, and children were noisily gathered outside the jail. Czechoslovak residents congregated there, too. A few fist fights erupted, and mounted police charged in to break up the incipient riot.

At this moment, the deputies emerged from the building. One of them, Karl May, a Nazi with a well-deserved reputation as a street brawler, grabbed a Czechoslovak and started thrashing him. A mounted officer leaned out of his saddle, whacked May with his club, and arrested him. Six other deputies were also taken into custody, and a number of Nazis were manhandled by the police.

Once the politicians were identified, the police dropped charges and released them. But within hours the Nazis began circulating a story describing how the deputies, "on an errand of mercy," were "beaten with whips and clubs, and trod upon by police horses." According to them, it was a perfect example of "Czechoslovak perfidy" and "persecution."

The Mährisch-Ostrau disorders gave Sudeten leaders the excuse they needed to break off negotiations and to denounce the Fourth Plan—not for its content, but rather because Czechoslovak sincerity was questionable.

"It is impossible to deal with men of such despicable character. . . . There is no guarantee that the so-called Fourth Plan will be implemented, were we to accept it . . . ," a Sudeten leader declared.

Something about the Mährisch-Ostrau affair aroused the suspicion of even the most anti-Czechoslovak members of the Runciman mission. The disorder had been too pat, too convenient.

"I shouldn't be surprised if the Henlein crowd stirred up that whole business just to make the Czechs look bad," a British observer on Runciman's staff said.

He was right. The Mährisch-Ostrau incident had been a deliberate provocation. The Sudeten Nazis knew they could start a brawl easily enough and, using it as a dodge to break off negotiations, they won time to receive Berlin's instructions about the Fourth Plan.

The orders from Germany were explicit. When this incident blew over, incite another one and another after that; keep putting off the negotiations and avoid any agreements.

"You will not have much longer to wait, comrades," a Nazi official assured Sudeten leaders.

Czechoslovak acquiescence made it difficult for the Sudeten

89

Germans to stall further, however. On September 9, the Prague government punished the police involved in the riot. The police chief of Mährisch-Ostrau resigned; the officer who had struck Deputy May was fired; several other policemen were suspended without pay. President Benes wrote letters of apology to May and the other deputies. He then asked the Sudeten Nazi leaders to resume negotiations.

He was told that most of them were attending a party rally at Nuremberg, Germany, but would be back in Czechoslovakia on Tuesday, September 13, after Hitler's scheduled speech of September 12.

More trouble was to break out before then. Benes addressed the nation by radio on Saturday, September 10. His theme was that the Fourth Plan would improve and increase democracy in Czechoslovakia. He called upon the people to remain calm and urged co-operation between Sudeten and Czechoslovak.

Incidents and disorders must be avoided, Benes said, strict discipline was needed. The Czechoslovak people must stand united as never before. "Hold together and we shall win!" he cried. "Hold fast and the nation will survive! Czechs, Sudetens, Slovaks, men of all the nationalities and minorities, stand firm! Democracy shall yet triumph!"

The Sudeten Nazi response to this appeal was a rash of riots on Sunday. In Eger, Nazi mobs assaulted Jews and Social Democrats. Before the uproar subsided eighteen anti-Nazis and thirteen policemen had been injured. In another town, Reichenberg, a Nazi crowd chased the police off the streets, broke up a Social Democratic party meeting, and attacked a number of people. Police reserves had to be called in to restore order.

That weekend, Lord Runciman was staying at the opulent castle of a former Austrian nobleman with a comic opera name—Count Ottokar Czerin von und zu Chudenitz. The count, a Nazi sympathizer, had helped plan an unusual divertisement for his distinguished British house guest.

On Sunday night, there appeared on the castle grounds a throng of Sudetenlanders. Some carried swastika banners, many wore the uniform of the Free Corps. A band played martial airs as the Sudetenlanders paraded around the courtyard. Runciman and his host came out on the balcony. The demonstrators lit pine torches and held them aloft; by the spluttering light they sang the Nazi anthem, the "Horst Wessel Song," and shouted *"Heil* Runciman! *Seig heil!,"* changing that cry to *"Heil* Hitler! *Seig heil!"*

Then they called upon the mediator for a speech. In German, Runciman said: "Men and women of Bohemia! You live in a beautiful country—perhaps one of the world's most beautiful. May God grant that this beautiful country have peace and that you will continue to live in it, in unity."

These insipid words aroused an ecstatic response. When at last the noisy mob stomped off behind the band, Runciman, moved by the "spontaneous" ovation, told Count Chudenitz, "I shall do everything to help this simple folk." But even as the mediator spoke, the "simple folk" were loosing a wave of terror throughout the Sudetenland.

The upsurge of disorder during the September 10 weekend caused great concern in Whitehall and the Quai d'Orsay. At any moment, the rioting might lead to insurrection and civil war in Czechoslovakia. French and British statesmen feared that the explosion could come if Hitler touched off the fuse in his Nuremberg address.

Thousands upon thousands of Nazis flocked to that city for the rally. "They come like pilgrims to Mecca," a Canadian newsman cabled his paper from Nuremberg. "Flags, banners, bands and uniforms, have flooded this ancient city. . . . On every side one sees men and women of the Labor Front, the Hitler Youth, the SS, SA, uniformed Nazi satraps with a confusing array of insignia and decorations . . . this huge mass of humanity awaits the arrival of Hitler as devout Christians look for the Second Coming. . . ."

At last the Fuehrer appeared. Standing in the back of a touring limousine, he drove through streets packed with his followers. The strutting, mustached little man who had once been labeled the "Austrian clown," held his right arm out stiffly in the Nazi salute and glared with burning eyes at the cheering, screaming thousands who paid him homage.

"Heil Hitler! *Seig heil!"* they roared.

Young women strewed flowers before his car. Scores of them, overcome at the sight of the Fuehrer, fainted on the spot. Hitler stood stern and unmoving; not a flicker of feeling crossed his face.

91

He was the Fuehrer; he was the warrior chieftain; he was Siegfried; he was the savior of Germany.

At 2:30 P.M., Monday, September 12, Hitler mounted the podium in the grandstand of the Nuremberg sports stadium and faced the microphones that would carry his speech by short wave radio to the rest of the world. Massed on the field were numberless Nazis. The banners of their groups and organizations flapped red in the sunlight, reminding one observer of a "gigantic pool of blood."

Seated in the guest section of the stand were the British, Italian, French, United States, Czechoslovak, and Russian envoys, as well as ambassadors and ministers from many other countries. More than two hundred newspaper and radio men were there to cover what one cynic called "the Nazi circus." Every seat was taken; every inch of space on the field was occupied.

At last Hitler spoke. The British ambassador, Sir Neville Henderson, must have shuddered at his words. To keep peace, no one had worked harder for the appeasement of Hitler than had Henderson; but the speech was a call to arms, full of bluster and menace, an incitement to war. The Czechoslovaks were depriving the Sudetenlanders of the very "right to live" and persecuting German "blood brothers" beyond endurance, Hitler shrieked. Like savage beasts, the Czechoslovaks "annihilated" and "massacred" innocent Sudetenlanders.

"From Germany, these poor people shall receive help and justice," the Fuehrer ranted. "I warn the world! I shall not be content forever to look on while the filthy Czechs oppress Germans! I say that the oppression shall cease! I say that the self-determination which was denied by the Versailles Treaty—the accursed Versailles Treaty—shall be given our brothers in the Sudeten. I warn the world! The Germans in Czechoslovakia are neither defenseless nor deserted. The German Father will not forsake his sons and daughters!" Hitler's tirade was greeted by a deafening ovation.

The response in the Sudetenland was not limited to cheers and applause. At the moment Hitler's speech ended, Nazis in every part of the region rose against the Czechoslovaks.

Rocks, bricks, and pieces of iron pipe shattered the windows of homes and businesses owned by Jews and Czechoslovaks. Free

Corps hoodlums looted and plundered the wrecked premises. The smoke of fires set by Nazi arsonists blackened the sky. Rioting broke out in more than seventy towns.

These were not spontaneous outbursts, but well-planned assaults. Prime targets everywhere were local and district police stations. Free Corps men, armed with German-made weapons, blasted away at beleaguered police trying to defend their headquarters.

Blood was shed on both sides as machine guns and rifles took a toll. Swastika flags were raised. Crowds screaming, "Down with Benes! *Heil* Hitler!" rushed through the streets. Battles raged all night and into the following day.

Reports of bitter clashes between police and Nazis flashed in Prague. Obviously, the uprisings were more serious than the ordinary Nazi-inspired disorders; they resembled full-scale revolt. It also became apparent that police could not cope with the mobs.

The Czechoslovak government acted promptly. Despite the danger of German intervention, Benes called out the Army and reservists. By the evening of September 13 (the day when negotiations were to be resumed with the Sudeten leaders), Czechoslovak troops had marched into the Sudetenland.

Within forty-eight hours, the soldiers had restored order; the Prague government once again controlled the Sudetenland.

Konrad Henlein, fearing arrest, fled into Germany. From that sanctuary, the Sudeten Fuehrer declared to the world: "The Sudeten Germans were forced into the Czechoslovak state against their will. The Czechs have refused a fair settlement because they hate the Sudetenlanders and seek to destroy them. We desire to live as free Germans, not Czech slaves! We wish to return to the Fatherland, to our beloved Reich! The hour has come to take up arms against the Czech murderers! May God give us strength and be with us in our righteous struggle!"

Allied leaders knew that Henlein would not have made such a bellicose statement unless he was backed by Hitler.

In Paris, Premier Daladier, who teetered from militancy to submission, from bubbling confidence to bleak despair, gave in to his apprehensions. On September 8, he had declared, "If a single German soldier crosses the Czech border, France will march to a man!"

The next day, the Premier, possibly inspired by his own boldness, called up reserves to complete their training. Troops due for release in September were ordered to remain on active service. Leaves were canceled. The Maginot Line received reinforcements. France approached a state of limited mobilization.

General Maurice Gamelin, the unpredictable French chief of staff, changed his tune and made optimistic predictions of a "grand offensive" in the event of war with Germany. His plans were more suited for 1916 than for 1938, however; all Gamelin could suggest was the same sort of bloody frontal assault that had cost so many French lives in the First World War.

The thought of German air strength depressed Daladier and threw Bonnet into panic. It was widely believed that Germany had eight thousand first-rate aircraft and could manufacture fifteen hundred more a month. This was greater than the combined aircraft output of Britain and France.

Faced with such facts at a time when Hitler was sounding increasingly militant, Daladier's resolution evaporated. He was overwhelmed by a vision of French cities pounded to rubble by German planes, while the French Army was bled white in futile offensives. Czechoslovakia was not worth such a price to France, the Premier decided. Somehow Hitler must be appeased.

In desperation, Daladier turned to Chamberlain. France would follow any policy Britain chose to pursue, but it was up to London to extricate Paris from the commitments to Prague.

"Get us out of the alliance," Daladier begged.

Neville Chamberlain was more than willing to oblige. Now he had a chance to demonstrate the efficacy of his appeasement policy. He would negotiate with Hitler on a face-to-face basis, not through an intermediary such as Runciman.

On September 13, Chamberlain sent an urgent message to Hitler:

In view of the increasingly critical situation I propose to come over at once to see you with a view to trying to find a peaceable solution. I propose to come across by air and am ready to start tomorrow. . . . Please indicate earliest time at which you can see me and suggest place of meeting. I should be grateful for a very early reply. . . .

94

In the days immediately preceding his request for a meeting with Hitler, Chamberlain had seen the powers approaching the brink of war. On September 13, that catastrophe seemed only hours away as reports of bloodshed and violence crackled over the wires from Czechoslovakia.

Neville Henderson, in Berlin, cabled the Prime Minister, warning that action must be taken immediately. "The severest pressures should be placed on Benes to force concessions for peace. . . . If this fails . . . it is my belief that Britain must act on its own, else nothing can head off a war. . . . I am persuaded that Hitler will march. . . ."

In Paris that day, lights burned late in the government offices along the Quai d'Orsay, as a despairing cabinet bickered over what to do. French leaders were divided on support to Czechoslovakia. At least three members of the cabinet—Auguste Champetier de Ribes, minister of pensions; Paul Reynaud, minister of finance; and Georges Mandel, minister of colonies, vigorously demanded that France fulfill all obligations to the Czechoslovaks. There were heated exchanges between Premier Daladier and Mandel.

"I will not sacrifice the entire youth of France merely to whitewash the criminal errors committed by you and the other members of the Big Four during the Peace Conference," Daladier shouted at the minister of colonies, in reference to the Versailles Treaty.

"But you will sacrifice the honor of France, because you are too craven to uphold it!" Mandel retorted.

Wringing his hands, Bonnet cried, "We cannot risk 10,000,000 Frenchmen to prevent 3,500,000 Sudetenlanders joining the Reich!"

The meeting broke up without achieving anything tangible, and Daladier admitted this impasse in a telephone call to Chamberlain, "I do not know what to do next!" the French Premier exclaimed. "I am at a loss!"

Chamberlain said nothing to the floundering Daladier of his decision to meet with Hitler. The Prime Minister fully realized the political risks he was taking, but felt that the effort must be made. As he later wrote: "The only alternative was war and I would never take that awful responsibility upon my shoulders unless it were forced upon me by others."

Somehow, he hoped it would be possible to persuade Hitler that force was not the answer to the Sudeten problem; somehow, he had to make the Fuehrer see that the matter could be settled through arbitration and negotiation. He would tell Hitler that the British intended to compel Benes to accept the decisions of an arbitrator whose judgment would be final and binding.

Without consulting his own cabinet, the Czechoslovaks, or the French, Chamberlain sent his request for a meeting with Hitler. The cable was delivered to the Fuehrer at Berchtesgaden on September 14. "I am thunderstruck!" the delighted Hitler confided to an aide. "Think of that! The Prime Minister of Great Britain is coming to entreat me! What a moment for Germany!"

In an uncharacteristically gracious gesture, Hitler invited both Chamberlain and his wife to come to Germany. (Mrs. Chamberlain did not accept.) The Prime Minister made the trip public during the afternoon of September 14. He accepted full responsibility for initiating it.

"In my heart I believe I am taking the correct path. I believe this is the road to peace. Millions of innocent people will be spared the horrors of war," Chamberlain said.

When the news of Chamberlain's scheduled meeting with Hitler broke over radio and in the newspapers, the rejoicing was almost universal. Nowhere was the enthusiasm greater than in England. A huge crowd converged outside the Prime Minister's residence at No. 10 Downing Street, singing "For He's a Jolly Good Fellow" and cheering Chamberlain lustily. An observer noted that there were more people on Downing Street than had gathered there at the time King Edward VIII abdicated.

Jubilation was somewhat muted in Paris, although thousands congregated at the British Embassy to shout, *"Vive* Chamberlain! *Vive la paix!"* French Communists and other anti-Nazis in the crowd chanted, *"À bas l'angleterre!* Down with England!" In typical Parisian style, a number of fights started.

Premier Daladier was relieved by Chamberlain's decision, but miffed that he had not been asked to accompany the British Prime Minister. Bonnet, who had always wanted deeper British involvement in the crisis, was delighted at the news of Chamberlain's journey, which won wide approval in official Paris. The French hoped Chamberlain would solve for them the dilemma of honoring their commitments and yet avoiding war.

96

Only in Prague was the British Prime Minister's flight looked upon with fear and suspicion. The Czechoslovak cabinet was bitter that Chamberlain had taken such a step without consulting them. "He's experimenting with our lives and making us his guinea pigs," a cabinet member said to a British newsman.

Jan Masaryk, the Czechoslovak ambassador in London, warned Prague that Czechoslovakia "might well have to pay a steep price for the senile ambitions of Chamberlain to act as the peacemaker to Europe. . . ."

CHAPTER 13

By mid-September, the Germans were fairly certain that they had little to fear from either Czechoslovakia's neighbors or her allies. Russia was showing signs of remaining aloof in the event of a Czechoslovak-German war; Great Britain and France seemed bent on preventing war at almost any price. Still, not even Hitler could be sure; the Western democracies and Russia might yet decide to fight.

But as Nazi war plans against Czechoslovakia were being rushed to completion, secret opposition to Hitler's schemes arose from an unlikely source—the German High Command, itself.

General Ludwig Beck, the Army chief of staff, was the ringleader of the "Generals' Plot." A supporter of Hitler in the beginning, Beck had turned cool toward the Fuehrer. He was concerned about Hitler's foreign policy and especially the Czechoslovak situation. Beck feared that an attack on Czechoslovakia would bring Britain, France, Russia, and eventually the United States, into a war against Germany. He also felt that the Wehrmacht could not hold the Westwall in the face of determined attacks by a hundred French divisions. In his opinion, Germany would not be ready for war until 1941.

With General Franz Halder, another high-ranking officer, Beck planned a *coup d'état*. Once the order had been given to invade Czechoslovakia, the several generals Beck and Halder had enlisted would go into action.

Hitler was to be arrested, charged with recklessly leading Germany to war, and brought before a People's Court, while the Army took over and set up a military dictatorship, to be replaced by a

99

civilian provisional government and then, at length, by a conservative democratic regime.

The military conspirators enlisted several diplomats in their scheme. The latter spoke to some British officials, trying to persuade them to make an outright declaration that an attack by Germany on Czechoslovakia would mean war. Such a stand, the German plotters averred, would stop Hitler. But even if it did not, the generals would act. They had the troops to overthrow Hitler. A bold, united front might deter him from war; if that failed, the military would get rid of him.

The generals were not acting out of high-minded motives. They had remained silent about the persecution of the Jews, the seizure of Austria, the destruction of the Weimar Republic. Until 1938, everything Hitler had done met their approbation. Under his leadership the Army, the Air Force, and the Navy had been rebuilt; from the 1918 defeat and the febrile years of Weimar, Germany had risen to a position of stability and power.

It was only because Beck and his colleagues felt that Germany was not yet ready to conduct a major war that they now opposed Hitler. They were against the war because they feared defeat; had victory been assured, the generals would not have hesitated to attack Czechoslovakia.

General Beck was a student of history. He could not believe that Britain and France would fail to intervene in a German-Czechoslovak war. He envisioned another 1918 for Germany, another humiliation, another Versailles Treaty. To prevent this, he felt he must stop Hitler.

Neither Beck nor his associates fully understood the politics of 1938. Hitler, on the other hand, was a brilliant political analyst; he correctly supposed that Chamberlain would sacrifice the Czechoslovaks to avoid war. If Britain failed to move, neither would France.

The swift flow of events that followed Chamberlain's offer to visit Hitler doomed the Generals' Conspiracy. Hitler achieved victory without war and by the time war really came, the generals were completely loyal to the Fuehrer.

One officer, General Wilhelm Adam, commanding German forces in the west, openly defied Hitler. When the Fuehrer made an inspection tour of the Siegfried Line early in September, Adam had a private talk with him.

He told the Fuehrer that it was impossible to hold the Siegfried Line with the troops at his disposal. "The man who does not hold these fortifications is a scoundrel!" Hitler replied. "I only regret that I am the Fuehrer and cannot be the supreme commander on the western front!"

General Adam did not long remain at his post. He was soon removed for reasons of "ill health" and retired from the service. General Beck and several of the other 1938 conspirators were involved in the 1944 plot against Hitler and were executed.

On September 15, 1938, only a fortnight before X-Day (invasion day) for Case Green, German plans for the attack on Czechoslovakia were complete. The same day Neville Chamberlain left London for his first meeting with the Fuehrer.

September 15 was a momentous day for sixty-nine-year-old Neville Chamberlain. As he prepared to embark on his first airplane flight he firmly believed that the fate of Europe—of the entire world—rested on the results of the journey.

Chamberlain was convinced that those who advocated going to war with Germany now rather than taking the chance of doing so later, were wrong. If his plan worked, there would be no war.

When Chamberlain left No. 10 Downing Street at 7:00 A.M. for Croydon Airport, he was surprised to see the street lined with admirers. "Good old Neville!" they cried. "Speak up to the Jerry!" "God bless, Chamberlain!" All the way to Croydon, there were cheering, waving throngs.

At the airfield, Chamberlain was escorted to a waiting plane—a Lockheed Electra, the fastest ship in the British airlines. A large crowd had gathered near the runway to bid him farewell. Among them were many notables, including Lord Halifax and the entire cabinet.

A steward took Chamberlain's baggage (an attaché case, a briefcase, and a small valise) aboard the plane. Mounting the steps of the ramp, Chamberlain posed for the photographers, flanked by the two aides who were to accompany him: Sir Horace Wilson and Sir William Strang, an official of the Foreign Office.

A battery of British Broadcasting Company (BBC) microphones had been set up and Chamberlain made a short statement: "I am going to see Chancellor Hitler because the situation seems to me of such a kind that discussions between him and me may have useful consequences. My policy has always been to ensure peace. The prompt acceptance of my suggestion encourages me to hope that my visit today will not be without results."

To the accompaniment of hearty applause and much hand-waving, Chamberlain and his colleagues entered the plane. The doors were closed, the ramp rolled away. Motors roared to life, propellers whirled, the pilot nosed his ship down the runway, and the Electra took off in bright sunlight. The time was 8:36 A.M.

Less than four hours later, as the city's church clocks were booming out the strokes of noon, the Electra swooped down at Oberweisenfeld, the Munich airfield. Foreign Minister Joachim von Ribbentrop was at hand to greet Chamberlain, Wilson, and Strang. Also present were Sir Neville Henderson and Paul Schmidt, the Nazi official interpreter.

After Henderson had made the introductions, Von Ribbentrop asked Chamberlain if he had a good flight. "Well, this is the very first one I ever made," the Prime Minister said, "so that I cannot judge whether or not it was good. The sun was shining when we left England. It was only when we got over the Continent that the clouds began."

Ribbentrop led the group to a Mercedes-Benz limousine which proceeded through the heart of Munich to the railroad station. Crowds stood three and four deep at the curb, pressing against police lines, cheering, waving, and calling out good wishes to the diplomats. Herr Schmidt informed Chamberlain, with evident satisfaction, that the public was far more enthusiastic than it had been when Mussolini visited Munich in 1937.

A special train, with steam up, was standing at the station siding, to carry the party on the three-hour trip to Berchtesgaden. Hitler had placed his private dining car at Chamberlain's disposal, and the men retired for lunch as the train pulled out. They were served a hearty meal—trout, roast beef and Yorkshire pudding, cheese, cakes, fruit, sherry, Rhine wine, German red wine, and port. At every railroad crossing, friendly crowds were waiting to wave at the visitors. But Chamberlain also saw trainloads of

102

troops, moving toward Czechoslovakia. The atmosphere in the luxurious dining car was genial. The diplomats talked about a variety of subjects—fishing, the scenery, the weather, anything and everything except the pressing issues at hand.

A limousine was waiting when the train pulled into Berchtesgaden. The car took them to Hitler's mountain hideaway—Berghof—the "Eagle's Nest." As the vehicle approached Berghof, rain began falling and a high, howling wind rose.

Hitler and General Wilhelm Keitel met the Britons on the steps leading to Berghof; handshakes were exchanged, and Hitler ushered them into a huge room where a glass wall looked out over the dreary, rainswept landscape.

This was the first time Chamberlain had ever seen Hitler. In a letter to his sister, Ida, written on September 19, 1938, the Prime Minister described his initial impression of the Fuehrer:

Halfway down these steps stood Hitler bareheaded and dressed in a khaki-colored coat of broadcloth with a red armlet and a swastika on it and the Iron Cross at his breast. . . . He wore black trousers such as we wear in the evening and black patent-leather lace-up shoes. His hair is brown, not black, his eyes blue, his expression rather disagreeable, especially in repose, and altogether he looks entirely undistinguished. You would never notice him in a crowd and would take him for the house painter he was. . . .

After being introduced to Strang and Wilson, Hitler suggested that they all have tea. While it was being served, the Fuehrer asked Chamberlain if he had any suggestions about procedure for the meeting.

The Prime Minister said he would like to make this a private discussion, with only Schmidt, the interpreter, present. He had been forewarned by Henderson that Von Ribbentrop might be a disruptive influence, since the Nazi foreign minister was an advocate of war. (Von Ribbentrop, angry at being excluded, later took petty revenge by refusing to let Henderson have a copy of notes of the talk as transcribed by Schmidt.)

During tea, the British Prime Minister had been rather shocked by the paintings of nudes which were hung around the large room.

103

They upset his sense of decorum. But in the room where Hitler and Chamberlain, accompanied by Schmidt, retired to confer, there were no paintings.

According to Chamberlain, "The place was completely devoid of decorations, lacking even a clock. On a pedestal table stood two bottles of mineral water and several glasses. A few chairs completed the furnishings." (Rather ruefully, Chamberlain recalled that Hitler had not offered him any of the mineral water.)

The conversation between the two leaders started off easily enough. Chamberlain declared that he had always sought better Anglo-German relations, but of late, as the Fuehrer well knew, these relations had deteriorated. Hitler listened impatiently. At the first chance, he broke in and launched a tirade against the Czechoslovaks.

"I will plunge the whole world into war to bring the Sudetenlanders home from Czechoslovakia," he declared. "On this point I will not yield! I shall choose my own time for an end to the persecution of Germans. Then, of course, the Czech question would be solved!"

At last, Chamberlain brought him up short with a sharp, "Hold on a minute!" Paul Schmidt later noted in his journal what happened next:

Surprised, for he was not used to being stopped like this, Hitler gazed at Chamberlain. . . . The British Prime Minister calmly said, "Let's get to the point, Herr Hitler. You say that the three million Sudeten Germans must be included in the Reich. . . ."

"That's right!"

"Would you be satisfied with that and there is nothing more that you want? I asked because there are many people who think . . . that you wish to dismember Czechoslovakia."

"If by that you mean that I want to include not only the Germans in the Reich but also Czechs, you are mistaken," Hitler said. "I don't want Czechs at any price! When the Sudeten Germans have returned to the Reich, the other minorities will want to secede in their turn—the Poles, the Hungarians, the Slovaks. . . . Believe me, what will be left of Czechoslovakia after that will be so small that I shall not have to worry about it any more!"

Having delivered this outburst, Hitler resumed his invective against the Czechoslovaks. In a voice that trembled with emotion, he repeated over and over again the barbarities Czechoslovaks had inflicted upon the Sudetens, pounding on the table as he recited the "atrocity" stories.

"I shall not tolerate such things any longer!" Hitler cried.

"Can we not make a joint appeal to both sides so that they may carry on with their talks in a calmer atmosphere?" Chamberlain asked.

"No! I'll not hear of it! An armistice between Czechs and Sudetenlanders is unthinkable. Czechs cannot be trusted. This whole business has been going on too long! Matters must be settled. I shall settle them myself, in one way or another. I'm ready to risk war rather than to see this state of affairs go on any longer!" Hitler replied.

Chamberlain, who had been calm to this point, now lost his temper. In quiet but icy tones, the British Prime Minister said, "If I have rightly understood you, Herr Hitler, you are determined to march against Czechoslovakia whatever happens. If this is what you meant to do, why did you let me come as far as Berchtesgaden? Under these conditions, the best thing for me to do is to go away again as quickly as I can. All this talk no longer seems to have any point."

Chamberlain rose as if to leave. But Hitler held up a restraining hand. If Britain would accept the principle of cession of the Sudetenland on the basis of self-determination it would be possible to avoid war. After all, there should be no objection, the Fuehrer sneered, self-determination was not his idea. The Allies had invented it to justify the provisions of the Versailles Treaty.

Chamberlain permitted himself a slight smile and returned to his seat. "At last," he said, "we are getting down to the crux of the matter."

Later, Chamberlain wrote, "I personally did not give two hoots whether the Sudetenlanders were in the Reich or out of it, according to their own wishes . . . but here was something practicable. I long had believed that the only solution was to detach the Sudeten areas from Czechoslovakia. . . ."

However, Chamberlain could not agree to grant this concession until he had consulted his government and secured the necessary permission to negotiate further on the question. The French, too, had to be informed, Chamberlain pointed out.

Hitler then told Chamberlain that he was sorry the Prime Minister would have to make another trip. "Our next meeting," the Fuehrer said, "will be arranged at a point closer to London than Berchtesgaden, so your journey will not be as tedious. . . ."

Chamberlain left the Berghof on September 16. He traveled to Munich by car, a pleasant ride in bright sunshine which contrasted sharply with the previous day's dismal weather. The Prime Minister was convinced that his visit had saved Europe from a war. Before parting with the Fuehrer, Chamberlain had exacted the promise that Hitler would not give the order for his armies to march unless "a completely impossible situation should arise. . . ."

Although Chamberlain did not like Hitler personally (he later described him as "hard and ruthless"), he believed the Fuehrer "was a man to be relied upon when he gave his word."

But as the Mercedes-Benz limousine was rolling toward the Oberweisenfeld airfield where Chamberlain's Electra stood poised for the flight back to England, Hitler made new adjustments in his campaign against Czechoslovakia.

By the time Chamberlain's plane was in the air, all German embassies had been notified: "The Fuehrer has stated to Chamberlain that . . . it no longer is a question of granting the Sudeten Germans autonomy, but solely of the cession of the Sudetenland to Germany. . . . Chamberlain had indicated his personal approval. . . ."

And as the Electra set down at Croydon, Hitler issued secret orders to five armies which included among their thirty-six divisions three armored divisions, giving them their jumping-off schedules for X-Day—October 1.

The Fuehrer also conferred with Hungarian representatives and urged them to demand an immediate plebiscite in the territories Hungary claimed, and to refuse to guarantee any proposed new frontiers for Czechoslovakia. Hitler made clear to the Hungarians that "when I finish this stew, there will be nothing left of the obnoxious Czechoslovak Republic. . . ."

The Fuehrer then called in the Polish ambassador and advised him to demand of the Czechoslovaks a plebiscite in the Teschen area. "You had better get what you can while the getting is good," Hitler commented cynically.

(The avaricious Poles rather mindlessly obeyed him. On September 21, less than a week after the Berchtesgaden meeting, the Poles demanded of the Prague government a plebiscite of the Teschen area where a good-sized Polish minority resided; at the same time, they sent troops up to that border. The next day, September 22, the Hungarians made similar moves. And on September 22, Sudeten Free Corps troops, backed by Nazi SS units, seized the Czechoslovak frontier towns, Asch and Eger, which jutted into Germany.)

Totally unaware of what Hitler was doing, Chamberlain stepped up to the microphones at Croydon airfield and reported: "I have had a frank but friendly talk with Herr Hitler. . . . I feel satisfied now that each of us fully understands what is in the mind of the other. . . . I must now report to the cabinet, and in a few days pay a return visit to Hitler. . . . He has graciously offered to come halfway to spare this old man another long journey. . . ."

Chamberlain then proceeded to a government Rolls-Royce and left the airfield for London, with cries of "Good Old Neville!" and "Well done, Neville!" ringing in his ears.

CHAPTER 14

On the evening of his return to London, September 16, Chamberlain reported to King George VI at Buckingham Palace. Thousands of Londoners had gathered outside the royal residence, and began shouting for the King and Chamberlain to appear on the balcony. When they did, the crowd gave them a tremendous ovation. The Prime Minister was understandably pleased by the favorable attention he had recently received; never before had he been a popular figure.

A special cabinet meeting was called for September 17 to hear Lord Runciman (who had been summoned from Prague) and Neville Chamberlain. The cabinet members were somewhat surprised at Runciman's recommendations. In his desire to satisfy the Germans, the mediator out-Hitlered Hitler. Runciman's proposals included the immediate transference of all predominantly German Sudeten areas to the Reich and the legal silencing in Czechoslovakia of all criticisms of Germany. He also proposed that the Czechoslovaks give assurances to their neighbors that under no circumstances would they "enter into aggressive action against them arising from obligations to other states. . . ."

The cabinet then listened to Chamberlain's account of his session with Hitler. The Prime Minister was eager for his advisers to support him unanimously in granting Hitler's demand for the cession of the Sudeten region to Germany.

Alfred Duff Cooper, the first sea lord, and Malcolm MacDonald, the colonial secretary, expressed their opposition to handing over the Sudetenlanders; nowhere in that territory was the population 100 percent German. What of the other minorities living there, they asked. Also, Duff Cooper objected vigorously to allowing one power—Germany—to dominate the continent of Europe. Only the first sea lord and MacDonald disputed Chamberlain, however. Britain would go along with the appeasement of the Nazis.

The next step for Chamberlain was to gain the acquiescence of the French. On September 16, even before the Prime Minister had returned from Berchtesgaden, Georges Bonnet informed Sir Eric Phipps, the British ambassador, that the French government would agree to any plan offered by either Chamberlain or Runciman, and would help impose it on Czechoslovakia. Should the Czechoslovaks object, Bonnet assured Phipps that France would consider her commitment to Czechoslovakia canceled. If Germany attacked, however, he announced with an air of bravado, France would "rush to the defense of the Czechoslovak nation."

Phipps astutely reasoned that Bonnet's last words were for public effect; he informed Chamberlain that France "does not intend to spring to the aid of Czechoslovakia" and advised the Prime Minister to gauge his decisions on that assumption, rather than on what Bonnet or Daladier might tell him.

With this in mind, Chamberlain invited the French Premier and foreign minister to London for consultations on Sunday, September 18. Before leaving Paris, Daladier, perhaps on the strength of a new burst of courage, called in the top generals of the French Army and asked them for a fresh appraisal of precisely what France could do against Germany without British help. The generals presented a pessimistic picture. The Germans would destroy the Czechoslovak Army in a few days. A French offensive could not be launched for at least three weeks; by then, a war to preserve Czechoslovakia would be useless. A similar opinion was expressed by the French cabinet with the exception of Mandel, Reynaud, and Champetier de Ribes.

Daladier's generals were frightened; his cabinet was split; the French people—except for the left-wingers—had no burning desire to fight for the Czechoslovaks. By the time the "Bull of the Vaucluse" flew to London with Bonnet, whatever lingering hope he might have had of rallying French support for a strong stand against Hitler was crushed.

110

Sunday, September 18, was marked by mass prayers to prevent war. In both England and France, the churches were jammed by anxious people who offered appeals to God to intercede for peace. From early morning, long lines of Londoners shuffled silently by the Tomb of the Unknown Soldier in Westminster Abbey, the symbol of Britain's sacrifice in 1914–18. At daybreak, Parisians congregated around the Eternal Light in the Arc de Triomphe; men, women, and children wept in memory of those who had fallen in the Great War, and prayed that a new conflict would not occur.

That overcast morning at 10:00 A.M., Bonnet and Daladier arrived at Croydon and were driven to No. 10 Downing Street in an official car. A police guard ringed the Prime Minister's residence to hold back the crowd gathered there and to deal with anti-Fascist demonstrators who shouted at the Frenchmen, "No concessions to Hitler!," "Stand by the Czechoslovaks!," "No Appeasement!"

Chamberlain opened the meeting with portentous news. He had been informed by Ambassador Jan Masaryk that Prague had decided to mobilize fully but would await the outcome of the Anglo-French talks. The Prime Minister then stressed his belief that the only way to avoid a catastrophe would be to comply with Hitler's demand for self-determination of the Sudetenland.

"I am convinced Herr Hitler can be trusted to keep his word and not march if we give him what he wants," Chamberlain said. "However, I know he will make war at once if we do not. The decision of war or peace rests with us!"

In this manner was the fate of the Czechoslovak Republic discussed; apparently neither the French nor the British considered it necessary for Prague to have a representative at the deliberations.

The French delegation as a whole was almost embarrassingly eager to accept any solution suggested by Chamberlain, but Daladier did not immediately agree to the cession of the Sudetenland on the basis of self-determination.

The Premier expressed token resistance on behalf of the Czechoslovaks, arguing that such a capitulation would open all central Europe to the Germans.

In bold-sounding phrases, he declared: "My colleagues and I

111

have come to London in the interest of peace, not to provide the means for the destruction of Czechoslovakia. If we accept self-determination for the Sudetenlanders, what would prevent German minorities in Rumania, Poland, and Slovakia from demanding first autonomy, then annexation by the Reich?"

To this Chamberlain responded patiently, "I have told you that Hitler will keep his word. The principle of self-determination will be applied only to the Sudetenland."

"No," Daladier cried, shaking his head. "I believe that every other minority in the Czechoslovak nation will raise the slogan of self-determination. Then we will have helped wipe out the country we created twenty years ago."

The discussion continued for hours, with breaks for lunch and dinner. Finally, at almost midnight, agreement was reached.

What emerged was a joint Anglo-French statement which stipulated that all territories whose populations were more than 50 percent Sudeten German must be turned over to Germany to assure "the maintenance of peace and the safety of Czechoslovakia's vital interests. . . ." For their part, Britain and France agreed to join in "an international guarantee of the new boundaries . . . against unprovoked aggression. . . ."

This guarantee, it was pointed out, would supplant the treaties the Czechoslovaks presently had with France, thus releasing the French from the burdensome responsibility of their pledge to defend Czechoslovakia. Daladier showed little enthusiasm over the conference's decision, but Bonnet was ecstatic. He exuberantly told a Danish reporter, "We are off the hook!"

As a sop to Czechoslovak feelings, the joint statement hypocritically expressed sympathy for Prague. It said in part:

Both the French and British governments recognized how great is the sacrifice thus required of the Czechoslovak government in the cause of peace. . . . But because that cause is common both to Europe in general and to Czechoslovakia in particular, they have felt it their duty jointly to set forth frankly the conditions essential to secure it. . . . Since Prime Minister Chamberlain must resume conversations with Herr Hitler no later than Thursday, September 22, and earlier if possible . . . we feel we must ask your reply at the earliest possible moment. . . .

The meeting ended at 12:15 A.M., September 19, and before parting with Chamberlain, Premier Daladier, who needed the approval of his cabinet, promised to get an answer from it by midday.

Daladier called an emergency cabinet meeting upon his return to Paris. He told his advisers that the Anglo-French proposal was the only way out of an "unpalatable mess."

In the event of war, he warned, France would have to fight alone for at least a month before British troops, in sufficient strength to matter, could be expected. Besides, the Luftwaffe had four thousand warplanes as compared to twelve hundred French, and should the French Army attempt to breach the Siegfried Line losses would be staggering.

The cabinet voted affirmatively for the Anglo-French plan. Mandel, Reynaud, and Champetier de Ribes also voiced their approval, but only because they believed the Czechoslovaks would turn down the proposal, forcing France to abide by its treaty with Prague.

Georges Bonnet, however, was determined that no such thing would take place. After the cabinet meeting, he told U. S. ambassador Bullitt, "If the Czechoslovaks refuse to go along with this, it will make no difference. I swear to you that France will not lift a finger to help Benes. He cannot refuse. We will not let Benes, in order to maintain the domination of seven million Czechs over 3½ million Germans, drive forty million Frenchmen to their deaths—and he knows it!"

Bonnet promptly summoned the Czechoslovak ambassador, Stefan Osusky, to the Quai d'Orsay. In unusually blunt and undiplomatic language, the French foreign minister broke the news to him. The Czechoslovak departed, brushing tears from his eyes. He told members of the press, waiting in the corridor, "My country has been condemned without a hearing. . . ."

In London, Lord Halifax received Masaryk, who listened to the proposal and then said coldly, "I was expecting an ultimatum from Berlin—but not from London and Paris. . . ."

During the afternoon of the same day (September 19), the British and French ambassadors to Prague, Sir Basil Newton and Victor-Leopold de Lacroix, presented President Benes with the Anglo-French proposal. Benes read the statement and looked up

113

in shock at his two visitors. "This is what you want? You have abandoned us!" he cried.

When Newton and De Lacroix protested that Britain and France were pledged to guarantee Czechoslovakia's new frontiers, Benes smiled wanly. "Will you guarantee my country's burial, as well?" he asked. "What you are proposing is not a solution to the problem. The cession of the Sudetenland marks only the first stage in the eventual dismemberment of Czechoslovakia by Germany. . . ."

After Newton and De Lacroix withdrew, Benes was left with a terrible decision. Accepting the Anglo-French proposal, he was convinced, meant ultimate occupation by the Germans; Hitler would never be satisfied with the Sudetenland alone. But Benes also knew that if he turned down his erstwhile allies, Czechoslovakia would have to face the Germans without assistance. As president of the Republic, did he have the right to risk the lives of his people in a hopeless battle? Was surrender less honorable than total destruction?

As Benes paced the floor of his suite in Prague's Hradschin Castle, the seat of the Czechoslovak government, he faintly heard from the street the sound of a huge crowd singing the national anthem. If the President doubted what must be done, the people suffered no such qualms. The Czechoslovak man-on-the-street was ready for war.

"Better death than the Germans!" a Prague newspaper headline shrieked. A high percentage of the population agreed.

CHAPTER 15

On September 20, Benes brought his cabinet together for its most important meeting in the republic's brief history. A bleak prospect faced the Czechoslovak statesmen, no matter what they decided. Certain war on the one hand; a tenuous peace on the other, with German domination likely in either case. No one doubted that the danger of war was real. The previous day members of the German legation in Prague began returning to Berlin.

As the members of the Benes cabinet hurried to Hradschin Castle, news flashed from the Sudeten frontier that units of Henlein's Free Corps had launched an attack on Czechoslovak troops entrenched along the border. The Free Corps thrust was easily fended off, although the Sudeten Nazis had enjoyed the support of German *panzers*. In a sense, war had already started when Benes called the cabinet session to order.

The meeting lasted many hours, but by midday, September 20, the British and the French had their answer. The Czechoslovaks rejected the Anglo-French proposal and appealed for the matter to be arbitrated as specified by the 1925 German-Czechoslovak treaty (which Hitler had abrogated long before).

In a dignified message, Kamil Krofta, the Czechoslovakian foreign minister, advised London and Paris of the cabinet's decision. His note explained that the Anglo-French terms had been turned down because acceptance of them would put Czechoslovakia "in the power of the Germans." Krofta's reply also reminded France of her treaty obligations and pointed out to the French their weakened position as a result of allowing Germany a free hand in central Europe.

115

The Czechoslovak response was received with ill grace in London and Paris. After hastily consulting via telephone, Chamberlain and Daladier ordered their envoys in Prague to apply "extreme pressure" on President Benes. The British and French diplomats were to warn the Czechoslovaks that no help of any sort could be expected if they continued to hold out.

By 1:30 A.M., September 21, Sir Basil Newton and Victor-Leopold de Lacroix had received final instructions from their Foreign Offices. Both hurried to Hradschin Castle for a consultation with Benes. The Czechoslovak President was wakened to face the diplomats. Each separately informed Benes that his government would leave the Czechoslovaks to their fate unless the Anglo-French proposals were unconditionally accepted. "If you do not do so," De Lacroix warned, "Czechoslovakia will be fully responsible for any war that may ensue and you can be assured that France will take no part in it."

The President argued frantically that Czechoslovakia could not accept the proposals; he indicated on a map how vital to the security of his country were the regions demanded by Germany. For more than an hour, Benes pleaded with the British and French ambassadors; Newton and De Lacroix listened in stony silence.

Finally, the weary President shrugged hopelessly and said, "You have given me an ultimatum. Either I do what you want, or you will stand by while the Germans trample us. I have no choice but to consult with my cabinet and recommend acceptance of your proposal. I will tell you this. France and Great Britain have grossly and disgracefully betrayed us."

At about 6:30 A.M., the Czechoslovak cabinet convened. Despite what Benes told them, the national leaders were reluctant to withdraw their rejection. Debate dragged on into midmorning. A few ministers, led by Premier Milan Hodza, wanted to give in, but a so-called "no surrender" bloc refused to yield.

Word of the cabinet standoff leaked out to Newton and De Lacroix. True to their instructions that "extreme" pressure must be put on Benes, the ambassadors sent a joint demand to the Czechoslovak President for an affirmative reply by noon, saying that otherwise their governments would no longer be responsible for what happened.

116

Even at this last moment, Benes had a glimmering of hope that a chance for outside support still existed. Vladimir Potemkin, Soviet deputy commissar for foreign affairs, at the behest of his superior, Maxim Litvinov, informed Benes that the Soviet Union "would bring Czechoslovakia . . . immediate assistance . . . in the event of a German attack, if France, true to her engagements, brought similar assistance. . . . The Soviet Union stands by Czechoslovakia in this hour of duress. . . ."

But the Russian message was merely a heartening gesture; under the treaty terms Stalin had no obligation to act until France did. The USSR ran no risks at all in promising to support the Czechoslovaks. Stalin was well aware that the French had abandoned the Czechoslovaks.

Another meaningless gesture came from the United States. President Roosevelt cabled that he "condemned" the stripping of territory from Czechoslovakia. He assured Benes of "sympathy and understanding" in the United States.

After hours of debate that often grew acrimonious, the cabinet meeting ended at 5:00 P.M. Bleary-eyed and disheveled, Krofta emerged from the conference room and summoned Newton and De Lacroix. He handed them the cabinet's decision. The statement declared that the Czechoslovak government, "forced by circumstances and pressures," now accepted the proposal outlined by the British and the French.

It did so "with the expectation" that both countries would safeguard "the vital interests of Czechoslovakia . . . now and in the future. . . ." The Czechoslovaks stressed the hope that they would be insured against German invasion even after the territory had been transferred and new frontiers fixed by an international commission upon which Czechoslovakia would have representation.

The appeasers had won a resounding triumph. Chamberlain could now bring Hitler "Czechoslovakia's scalp on a silver platter," as an American newspaperman put it.

There remained for Benes the melancholy chore of letting his people know what had happened. He also wanted the world to hear the conditions under which Czechoslovakia had been forced to surrender.

117

At about 7:00 P.M., a government spokesman released the news in a radio broadcast:

Our friends and allies have obliged us to accept conditions that are usually put forward to a beaten enemy. . . . It is not lack of courage that has forced us to take a decision that wrings our heart. . . . Let us not judge those who have deserted us at the moment of disaster—history will make her decision. . . .

The announcement set off furious demonstrations in Prague. Thousands upon thousands of patriotic Czechoslovaks poured into the streets. A huge crowd packed the square in front of the Hradschin Castle. "Down with the cabinet! Long live the Army!" the people chanted. *"We want to fight! We want to fight!"*

Late in the evening, General Jan Syrovy, the Army's inspector general, appeared on a balcony in an effort to calm the people. "My countrymen!" he began, "We cannot lead a whole nation to suicide . . . !"

At this a great roar from the crowd interrupted him, *"We want to fight!"*

Prague was in ferment. All night groups of men and youths roamed the streets singing patriotic songs. Crowded cafes and restaurants remained open and did a land-office business. Everywhere slogans were chalked on walls: "Down with Hodza!"; "Death before Dishonor!"; "Down with Hitler!"

Premier Milan Hodza, who had pressed for capitulation, realized his political career was over. He tendered his resignation on September 22, the day after he had sponsored Czechoslovakia's humiliation. A new government of "national safety" under General Jan Syrovy was formed, and President Benes, seeking to calm the people, spoke to them in a nationwide broadcast. After urging unity and fortitude during the "dark days ahead," the President said:

I have never feared, and I do not fear for the future of our nation. I have a plan for all circumstances, and will not allow myself to be led astray. . . . I see things clearly. . . . Have no fear for the nation and the state. . . . The nation has deep roots. Czechoslovakia will not perish!

118

The victory for appeasement was not greeted by universal acclaim in London or Paris. The Labor Party expressed its "profound humiliation" before this "shameful submission to Hitler" and deplored the fact that the "long British tradition of democracy should be flouted thus. . . ."

Winston Churchill, a Conservative, told a press conference:

The partition of Czechoslovakia under pressure from England and France amounts to the complete surrender of the Western Democracies to the Nazi threat of force. . . . The belief that security can be obtained by throwing a small State to the wolves is a fatal decision. . . . The war potential of Germany will increase far more rapidly than it will be possible for France and Great Britain to complete the measures necessary for defence. . . .

In Paris, left-wingers staged huge rallies. Hostile marchers raged through the streets, condemning Daladier, Bonnet, and all the other French leaders who had "sold out" the Czechoslovaks.

A Communist deputy, addressing a large crowd, cried: "As Frenchmen, we bow our heads in disgrace at the perfidy of the Daladier government! The dead of Verdun cry out at the disgrace today inflicted upon our country! Frenchmen! We have been betrayed! Down with Daladier! Down with Bonnet! Long live the *Fronte Populaire!* Death to Fascism!"

But to some, Neville Chamberlain was the apostle of peace. Many were grateful to him for having "the courage not to fight."

"It is easier to wage a war than to prevent one," a London newspaper editorialized. "At some future date, historians will evaluate properly and objectively, the great contribution to mankind made by Neville Chamberlain, who snatched the world from disaster. . . . Tonight we raise our glass in praise of Neville Chamberlain, warrior of peace. . . ."

18. Appearing slightly bilious, French Premier Edouard Daladier (r.) is met at Munich Airport by dapper German Foreign Minister von Ribbentrop, once a wine salesman. Daladier was a principal in the Munich Conference, September 29–30, 1938, which produced the notorious Munich Pact, sealing Czechoslovakia's fate. (USIA)

19. Prominent at the Munich Conference which included Britain, France, Germany, and Italy was Benito Mussolini, shown with Nazi bigwigs (l. to r.) Hermann Goering, Heinrich Himmler, Rudolf Hess, and Adolf Hitler (back to camera). (ADN/ZENTRALBILD)

20. Wearing a Fascist militia uniform bedecked with rows of campaign ribbons, the massive-jawed Duce listens as Prime Minister Chamberlain stresses a point between Munich Conference sessions. Mussolini's martial dress is in sharp contrast to Chamberlain's formal diplomatist's attire. (UPI)

21. The talks ended, delegates affix their signatures to the Munich Pact: Chamberlain squints through old-fashioned pince-nez glasses. (UPI)

22. Daladier shows his distaste for the document. (UPI)

23. Hitler scribbles his signature hastily as Mussolini and Goering chat in the background. (UPI)

24. Il Duce forcefully scrawls his name...and the betrayal of Czechoslovakia is an accomplished fact. (UPI)

25. The Big Four: Chamberlain, Daladier, Hitler, and Mussolini stand together uneasily after the pact signing. Photo was taken in the conference room of Munich's ornate Fuehrerhaus, where the parley was held. (UPI)

26. A black-uniformed SS guard presents arms as Nazi and Fascist chieftains leave the Fuehrerhaus early in the morning of September 30, at the close of the conference. Seen are Mussolini, Hitler, Goering, and Il Duce's son-in-law, Count Galeazzo Ciano (behind Hitler). (UPI)

We, the German Führer and Chancellor and the British Prime Minister, have had a further meeting today and are agreed in recognising that the question of Anglo-German relations is of the first importance for the two countries and for Europe.

We regard the agreement signed last night and the Anglo-German Naval Agreement as symbolic of the desire of our two peoples never to go to war with one another again.

We are resolved that the method of consultation shall be the method adopted to deal with any other questions that may concern our two countries, and we are determined to continue our efforts to remove possible sources of difference and thus to contribute to assure the peace of Europe.

[signature: Adolf Hitler]

[signature: Neville Chamberlain]

September 30. 1938.

27. Without revealing his intentions to anyone, Chamberlain met Hitler secretly on September 30 at the Fuehrer's Munich apartment. The unscheduled talk resulted in the agreement reproduced here. (USIA)

28. After reaching their bilateral accord, Chamberlain and Hitler wearily face the camera. The Prime Minister left for England a few hours later, convinced that he had secured lasting peace for Europe and the whole world. (UPI)

29. Upon his return home from Munich on September 30, Chamberlain waves a copy of the "no war" agreement with Hitler and tells a happy airport crowd, "I believe it is peace for our time." Less than a year later, the Second World War broke out. (WIDE WORLD)

30. Many Englishmen disagreed with Chamberlain's policy of appeasement. Dissenters in London's Hyde Park prod giant caricature of the Prime Minister with spears bearing the names of groups opposed to his government. (UPI)

CHAPTER 16

As soon as the Czechoslovaks had agreed to the Anglo-French ultimatum, Chamberlain arranged to meet Hitler again. The time of the meeting was to be Thursday, September 22, at 3:00 P.M.; the place, the Hotel Dreesen in Godesberg, an attractive spa resort on the Rhine River near Bonn and Cologne.

On the day of the Godesberg conference, violence broke out in the Sudetenland as Czechoslovaks and Free Corps men clashed. It was rumored that thirty German divisions were on the move toward the Czechoslovak frontier. Despite warnings from London and Paris, the Czechoslovak government under General Syrovy announced that it would commence full mobilization unless the Free Corps ceased its provocations.

At Croydon Airport radio microphones and newsreel cameras recorded Chamberlain's departure for Godesberg. As the Lockheed Electra warmed up on the runway, the Prime Minister addressed the crowd.

"A peaceful solution of the Czechoslovakian problem is an essential preliminary to a better understanding between the British and German peoples; and this, in turn, is the indispensable foundation of European peace. European peace is what I am aiming at and I hope this journey may open the way to get it," Chamberlain said. Observers noted that his face was grim and lined with worry.

Having delivered this statement, the elderly statesman climbed slowly up the ramp steps. At the door of the plane, he turned and waved his furled umbrella to the cheering onlookers.

Accompanying the Prime Minister on this trip were Sir Horace

121

Wilson, William Strang, Sir Neville Henderson, Ivone Kirkpatrick, a Foreign Office interpreter, and Sir William Malkin, the head of the Foreign Office legal department. (Because Von Ribbentrop had refused him the notes taken by Schmidt, Chamberlain had brought along his own official interpreter this time.)

After an uneventful two-hour flight, the Electra put down at Cologne's airfield at 12:27 P.M. Even before the plane took off, the German *chargé d'affaires* in London had warned his Foreign Office that the Godesberg meeting might run into trouble. "The British Prime Minister and his party have left under a heavy load of anxiety. . . . Unquestionably, opposition is growing to Chamberlain's policy. . . ."

This knowledge did not dampen the elaborate reception the Nazis had readied for Chamberlain, however. Dozens of German dignitaries, headed by Von Ribbentrop, were waiting at the runway. A band blared "God Save the King" and *"Deutschland über alles."* An honor guard of elite troops presented arms smartly in salute to the Britons as Chamberlain's party descended from the aircraft. A crowd numbering several thousand pressed against the high wire fence that surrounded the airfield. At the sight of the Prime Minister, the spectators burst into prolonged applause and cheering.

Chamberlain had not expected such an enthusiastic reception. A smile creased the Prime Minister's face and he waved his umbrella in response to the ovation.

The Englishmen were shepherded to limousines. Behind a motorcycle escort of Cologne policemen, the motorcade, sirens shrieking, rolled away from the airfield.

The road into Cologne was lined with friendly crowds, waving and calling out to the visiting statesmen. Schoolchildren had been given a holiday and they stood in groups, waving small German and British flags. White-aproned high school girls tossed flowers at the car that carried Chamberlain and his colleagues.

On through Cologne went the cavalcade; in the ancient city, bells pealed, bands played, and onlookers shouted their welcome.

The automobiles crossed to the west bank of the Rhine at Bonn and proceeded to the Hotel Petersberg in Godesberg. The hotel was a magnificent one. From its balconies could be seen the

122

equally magnificent Hotel Dreesen on the other side of the river where Hitler awaited his guest.

The rooms prepared for the British delegation were both elegant and luxurious. Fruit, cigars, and cigarettes had been provided for the visitors as well as brandies, liqueurs, and whiskies.

Herr Dreesen, who also owned the Hotel Petersberg, was an old war comrade of Hitler. He had prospered under the Nazi regime and was the proprietor of factories that manufactured eau de cologne, hair lotion, shaving soap, and bath salts. Generous samples of these products had been provided for the Englishmen.

If the warm reception and opulent accommodations had lulled Chamberlain and his colleagues, the Fuehrer, in the Hotel Dreesen, was far from pleased. He paced nervously, great black rings shadowing his eyes.

Hitler had been infuriated by the Czechoslovaks' initial refusal to accept the Anglo-French proposals. It was rumored that Prague's stand had thrown Hitler into such a maniacal mood that, in a fit of rage, he had thrown himself on the floor and chewed the edges of the carpet.

One American newsman, William L. Shirer, observing him at breakfast in the Hotel Dreesen, noted that the Fuehrer "seemed to be . . . on the edge of a nervous breakdown. . . ."

When Chamberlain and his party, refreshed after a sumptuous lunch, left the Petersberg for the Dreesen, church clocks in Godesberg were ringing out four o'clock. The Englishmen crossed to the Rhine's eastern shore on a ferry boat escorted by police launches.

The British walked from the landing to the hotel lobby, which was crowded with Nazi officials wearing a variety of uniforms. In a few minutes, someone announced, "The Fuehrer is coming!" Surrounded by his bodyguard of SS troopers, Hitler appeared and greeted Chamberlain. The Prime Minister and the Fuehrer chatted briefly, then proceeded to a conference room on the first floor, accompanied by Paul Schmidt and Ivone Kirkpatrick, the official interpreters.

The meeting chamber was large; its windows opened onto a balcony with a splendid view of the Rhine River and the mountains beyond. Paul Schmidt observed that neither of the statesmen "had a mind for all that beauty . . . without even glancing at the

123

landscape they at once sat down at a long table covered with green cloth. . . ." Hitler sat at the head, with Chamberlain on his right, and the interpreters—Schmidt and Kirkpatrick to the left.

Moments passed in absolute silence, and then Hitler gestured for Chamberlain to begin. The British Prime Minister gave the Fuehrer a complete account of what had happened since the Berchtesgaden session. After reviewing the "laborious negotiations" with France and Czechoslovakia, Chamberlain said, "I have succeeded in causing not only the British and French cabinets, but also the Czechoslovak government, to accept in principle what you asked of me during our last conversation."

The Prime Minister then went on to describe at length the procedure by which the Sudetenland should be ceded to the Reich. He discussed the need of compensation for all public and private property to be taken over by Germany. The security of the new Czechoslovak frontiers was inviolate, Chamberlain declared. "France and Great Britain will give their guarantee to this. . . . And I hope that for her part, Germany—since as you have told me, she will no longer have any fresh territorial claim to express —will agree to sign a nonaggression pact with Czechoslovakia."

Having delivered his report, Chamberlain sat down, looking, as Schmidt reported, like ". . . a man smugly satisfied with his accomplishments. . . ."

That complacency was rudely shattered by the Fuehrer. When Chamberlain had finished, Hitler sat frowning at the green table covering. He looked up and calmly asked, "Then, I am to understand that the British, French, and Czech governments have agreed to the transfer of the Sudetenland to Germany?"

"Yes, you are correct," Chamberlain replied.

Again Hitler fell silent, his brow furrowed as though he were wrestling with a tremendous decision. Finally, he spoke, in a firm, decisive tone. "I am exceedingly sorry, Herr Chamberlain, but that is no good. It is no longer of any use. I very much regret I am not able to accept these things, but after the events of the last five days, this solution is no longer adequate!"

Chamberlain's face flushed with anger. In a barely controlled voice he said, "What do you mean? Everything you asked for at Berchtesgaden has been done! Do you imagine I am going back to London with new proposals? I would be laughed out of office!"

124

Hitler answered calmly, showing no emotion. Kirkpatrick remembered that his voice "was unnatural." He told Chamberlain that there could be no true settlement of the Czechoslovak question while Poland and Hungary still demanded satisfaction. In the past five days, he explained, representatives of those two countries had made known to him their claims on the Czechoslovaks.

Chamberlain was shocked. "You are playing a wicked game, Herr Hitler," he said. "Did you not tell me yourself that the Poles and the Hungarians had nothing to do with the Sudeten question? You insisted that German demands must be satisfied before anything could be done about any other claims against the Czechoslovaks. And now you raise this very point!"

"Your proposals on the settlement of the Sudeten problem involve too long a delay," Hitler replied. "An end must be put to it at once. The German Army must immediately occupy the Sudeten territory ceded to Germany!"

Then Hitler's composure crumbled and he launched into a tirade against Benes, the Czechoslovaks, the Versailles Treaty, and the mistreatment of Germany over the past twenty years.

After three hours, the first session of the Godesberg Conference ended, as Hitler and Chamberlain mutually consented to an adjournment. No agreement had been reached and none seemed likely. Several times during the session war had seemed inevitable. But as they neared the precipice, both men veered off to safer ground.

Chamberlain left Hitler at 7:15 P.M. and, with his party, was driven to the river ferry between ranks of German civilians still smiling, still waving, still cheering the Britons.

The Prime Minister and his advisers retired at once to their Hotel Petersberg suite and spent the rest of the evening in consultation.

The reports coming in from the Czechoslovak frontier were far from reassuring; fighting was going on at several points between Prague troops and Free Corps detachments. According to the latest despatches, swastika flags had been raised over the towns of Asch and Eger. Tension prevailed throughout the region; as one observer wrote, "Nobody knows when these little explosions will set off a blast strong enough to shake the world. . . ."

125

In this uneasy atmosphere, Chamberlain and his aides discussed the situation and considered their next move. That night the British statesmen had little sleep.

While breakfasting the next morning on his balcony, Chamberlain informed his colleagues that rather than meet with Hitler again, he would write the Fuehrer a letter; perhaps the air might be cleared so that any future talks would prove fruitful.

Chamberlain wrote in part:

The difficulty I see about the proposal you put to me yesterday afternoon arises from the suggestion that the area should in the immediate future be occupied by German troops. . . . Even if I felt it right to put this proposal to the Czechoslovak government, I am convinced that they would not regard it as being in the spirit of the arrangement which we and the French government urged them to accept . . . and which they have accepted. . . . In the event of German troops moving into the areas as you propose, there is no doubt that the Czechoslovak government would have no option but to order their forces to resist. . . .

The Prime Minister went on to write that public opinion in France and Great Britain would condemn the presence of German troops as "an unnecessary display of force." Since all parties had agreed on the transfer of the Sudeten areas to Germany, however, Chamberlain was willing to suggest to Prague that the Sudeten Germans themselves maintain law and order until the region was turned over to Germany.

The letter was carried to the Hotel Dreesen by Sir Horace Wilson and Ivone Kirkpatrick. They delivered it at 10:00 A.M., but no reply came from Hitler until about 3:00 P.M. when Schmidt emerged from the Dreesen carrying a brown envelope. He climbed into a Mercedes and headed for the ferry, his appearance causing a flurry among newsmen and spectators. When Schmidt's car drew up to the Hotel Petersberg, the interpreter was almost mobbed by reporters. It took several husky policemen to force a way for Schmidt, who strode on, clutching the envelope and refusing to answer any questions. Just as he disappeared into the hotel, a reporter shouted in exasperation, "Well, at least tell us if it's war or peace! We can't stand the suspense!"

126

CHAPTER 17

If excitement was boiling around the Hotel Petersberg, no one could tell it from Chamberlain's appearance. "The old man seemed unruffled, completely at ease, looking for all the world like an elderly visitor enjoying a vacation," an observer noted.

The Prime Minister received Schmidt graciously and made small talk while the edgy interpreter literally "hopped from one foot to the other," fingering the brown envelope that contained Hitler's message.

At last Chamberlain accepted the envelope and drew out a long letter which Schmidt promptly translated for him. The contents proved disappointing; Hitler harped on the wrongs done by the Czechoslovaks to Germans, refused to modify his position, and concluded that war "now appears to be the case." He did present certain proposals, however, among them:

1. The Sudetenlanders must be returned to Germany under the right of self-determination.

2. To enable changes to be made in the frontier lines, Hitler was willing to permit a plebiscite in territories where less than 50 percent of the inhabitants were German. Such a plebiscite was to be held under the auspices of either an international commission or a German-Czech commission.

3. The Fuehrer agreed to withdraw German troops from the disputed areas during the plebiscite if the Czechs did the same. The maintenance of order, however, could not be entrusted to the German Sudetenlanders; instead, perhaps a mixed German-Czech police force could be created.

If the principle that the Sudetenland really belonged to the Reich was accepted by all concerned, Hitler could see no reason for a delay. It was then that he wrote, "If Germany . . . cannot have the rights of the Sudetenlanders recognized by negotiations . . . other means will be used . . . including war, which now appears to be the case. . . ."

After about an hour, Schmidt departed for the Hotel Dreesen, once again running the gantlet of newsmen.

Hitler had been anxiously awaiting Schmidt's return. When the interpreter entered the Fuehrer's suite, Hitler grabbed him by the arm and asked, "What did Chamberlain say? How did he take my letter?"

"Herr Chamberlain did not seem upset or disturbed," Schmidt said. "He told me that in about an hour or so, Henderson and Wilson would bring you his reply."

The two Englishmen arrived promptly and gave Hitler Chamberlain's note. It stated:

In my capacity as intermediary, it is evidently now my duty—since Your Excellency maintains entirely the position you took last night—to put your proposals before the Czechoslovak government. . . .

Accordingly, I request . . . you to let me have a memorandum which sets out these proposals, together with a map showing the area proposed to be transferred . . . subject to the result of the proposed plebiscite. . . . I shall then return to England. . . . I do not see that I can perform any further service here. . . . I will forward your memorandum to Prague and request the reply of the Czechoslovak government at the earliest possible moment. . . .

Wilson and Henderson waited for a reply, after being asked by Von Ribbentrop to do so.

Chamberlain's failure to call for a second meeting with Hitler had caused some consternation among the Nazis. Not all of the Fuehrer's closest advisers were yet fully committed to war. The "moderates" sought to convince Hitler that he should not let Chamberlain go away without another personal meeting.

In view of the high hopes the German public had placed on the

128

Godesberg talks, Hitler himself was reluctant to break off negotiations. It was one thing to bluster about war, and another actually to launch one; even the Fuehrer saw that war made no sense if he could get what he wanted without fighting for it.

Accordingly, he instructed Von Ribbentrop to inform Henderson and Wilson that he wished another meeting with Chamberlain. The Germans would prepare the requested memorandum and inform the British when it was ready to be discussed.

At 10:00 P.M. Von Ribbentrop telephoned the Hotel Petersberg to advise Chamberlain that the Fuehrer would be ready to see him in half an hour. Back across the river hastened the Prime Minister, accompanied by his entire entourage.

Hitler greeted Chamberlain cordially in the Hotel Dreesen lobby and then guided him to a large drawing room on the building's ground floor. Due to the gravity of the situation both leaders had their staffs with them. Neither Chamberlain nor Hitler cared to assume sole responsibility for the outcome of this session.

Speaking softly and diplomatically, Hitler opened the proceedings by saying, "Although it has been difficult to find a basis of agreement, I hope that it is still possible for us to find a peaceful solution. . . ."

Chamberlain was amazed at the change in Hitler's manner from the evening before, when he had acted like a madman. The Prime Minister also expressed hope that the Czechoslovak crisis could be settled amicably and asked to see the German memorandum.

As he handed the papers to Chamberlain, Hitler said, "Here you will find the substance of the ideas and suggestions that I spoke of during our last interview."

The memorandum boiled down to six points:

1. The evacuation of all Czechoslovak troops, police, gendarmes, customs officials, and frontier guards from territory marked on the accompanying map as due to be transferred. This area is to be handed over to the Germans between September 26–28.

2. The evacuated territory must be handed over in the condition which it is at present (September 23).

3. All Sudetenlanders serving in the Czechoslovak army or police must be honorably discharged at once and sent home.

129

4. The Czechoslovak government must free all prisoners of German race who have been arrested for political acts.

5. The German government agrees that a plebiscite shall take place in territories that are to be determined between now and November 25 at the latest. The frontier adjustments arising as the result of this plebiscite will be decided upon either by a Czech-German or an international commission.

All persons residing in the areas in question on October 28, 1918, or born there prior to that date, are eligible to vote.

The simple majority of the . . . persons entitled to vote shall be held to express the desire of the population to belong to the German Reich or the Czechoslovak State.

6. The German government proposes the setting up of a Czech-German committee with power to settle all other details.

Added to these demands was an appendix which spelled out the conditions of the transfer:

The handing over of the evacuated Sudeten territory must take place without the military, economic, or transport installations having been destroyed or made unusable; the same applies to airfields and other ground installations and all radio stations. . . . Economic and transport material . . . particularly rolling stock, must be handed over intact. The same applies to all public service plants and equipment, i.e.: gasworks, electric generating equipment, etc. Lastly, there must be no removal of supplies, personal estate, cattle, raw materials, etc.

When Schmidt translated this to Chamberlain, the British Prime Minister cried out, "This is an *ultimatum!* Not a *memorandum!*"

Hitler smiled unpleasantly. ("A smile that curdled one's blood," an observer recalled.) "But, Herr Chamberlain, as you see, this paper is headed 'Memorandum,' not 'Ultimatum,'" he replied.

"I attach more importance to the contents than the title," Chamberlain said stiffly, ignoring Hitler's attempt at humor. "This document is couched in the terms of a conqueror to the conquered."

130

Just then, an aide rushed in with a dispatch for the Fuehrer. Hitler read the message and passed it on to Schmidt. "Translate this for Herr Chamberlain," he ordered.

Schmidt read: "Benes has just announced over the radio a general mobilization in Czechoslovakia."

(The interpreter later noted: "After the big-drum bang of Czech mobilization there were two or three long bars of silence. . . .")

Hitler, who seemed "thunderstruck," said, "Now, of course, the whole affair is settled! But despite this provocation, I still hold to my promise to undertake nothing against Czechoslovakia during the negotiations, or at least while you are still on German soil, Herr Chamberlain."

Hitler's attitude angered Chamberlain. "The Czechs have good reason to mobilize," he snapped. "After all, Germany mobilized first."

The Fuehrer's eyes glared wildly at the gaunt Englishman. "That is not so! The day Germany mobilizes, you will see the meaning of mobilization!"

But in spite of the Czechoslovak mobilization and the ensuing arguments about it, the conference did not break up. The talks dragged on until early morning. At last, Chamberlain demanded, "Is this memorandum really your last word, Herr Hitler?"

"*Ja!* It is," the Fuehrer replied.

"In that case," Chamberlain said, "there is no further purpose in continuing these conversations. I shall return to England with a heavy heart, for I have seen the wreck of all my hopes for peace in Europe. But I go with a clear conscience. I have done everything possible for peace. . . ."

When it became apparent that Chamberlain was actually about to leave, Hitler again grew conciliatory. If it would help, the Fuehrer said, he would tone down his memorandum, remove the phrases which gave it the effect of an ultimatum.

And as a special gesture to Chamberlain he declared magnanimously, "For you, Herr Prime Minister, I am going to change the date of the occupation. I shall agree that the ceded territories be turned over to Germany by October 1, rather than September 28, as stated. You may take pride, Herr Chamberlain, in knowing that you are the only man to whom I ever have offered a concession. Once my mind is made up, I never change it."

According to observers, Chamberlain was highly pleased by this "victory" over Hitler. The Prime Minister was unaware that he had gained nothing; that October 1 was the date originally set for the invasion of Czechoslovakia in Case Green. He was convinced that the proposed three-day "delay" indicated Hitler's "good will."

In his turn, Chamberlain, who had refused earlier to pass the memorandum on to the Czechoslovaks, reversed himself after Hitler altered some of its wording and changed the date. He told the Fuehrer, "It is not for me either to accept or reject your proposals. . . . As an intermediary, the most I can do is place them before the Czechoslovak government. . . ."

This suited Hitler perfectly. If the Czechoslovaks now refused to accept his terms, they would be blamed for turning down a "peaceful" solution and choosing instead to make war.

Chamberlain and Hitler parted at 2:00 A.M. The Fuehrer warmly thanked Chamberlain for all his efforts and in a voice that rang with sincerity, repeated his promise that the Sudeten question was "the last big problem" he had to settle. Chamberlain evidently believed him.

When the Prime Minister returned to the Hotel Petersberg, a journalist asked, "Is it hopeless, sir? Will there be a war?"

"I would not like to say that," Chamberlain replied. "It's all up to the Czechs now."

CHAPTER 18

While Chamberlain and Hitler were meeting at Godesberg, the Czechoslovaks mobilized in self-defense. At 10:30 P.M., the Prague radio station had interrupted its regular program for a special announcement.

A government spokesman calmly said:

Citizens: general mobilization has been ordered. All men aged less than forty years of age and specialists of any age must rejoin their reserve units at once. . . .

The latest possible date for reporting . . . is September 24, at four-thirty in the morning. . . . All cars, trucks, aeroplanes, and other vehicles are declared mobilized for military use. . . .

Citizens: the decisive moment is coming. Let each man put all his strength at his country's disposal. Be brave and true. Ours is a struggle for justice and freedom. Long live Czechoslovakia!

This decree was read first in Czech, then in Slovak, German, Hungarian, and Ruthenian. At the end, the national anthem blared over the airwaves.

Immediately after the broadcast, spontaneous parades formed on the streets of Prague and singing crowds gathered in public squares. Reservists, wearing hastily donned uniforms, were escorted to the railroad depot by cheering citizens. Mobilized soldiers hurried to regimental armories and received arms and equipment.

So efficient was the mobilization that by morning, an astounded German military attaché notified Berlin: "Prague calm. Mobiliza-

133

tion smooth. Estimate more than 1,500,000 under arms. Field army about 850,000. People confident."

Military recruiting offices were besieged by Czechoslovaks over forty and thousands of foreigners seeking to volunteer for active duty. A high officer of the French military mission tore up his passport and reported to Czechoslovak Army headquarters, offering his services in any capacity, in any rank, although he wore a colonel's insignia.

No sooner had the mobilization order been given than lights were dimmed in Prague and other Czechoslovak cities; antiaircraft gunners manned their weapons; searchlight beams probed the skies. Czechoslovakia was braced for war.

A Dutch newspaperman in Prague, impressed by the manner in which the mobilization had come off, wrote:

The people here have no illusions about the trials awaiting them. . . . The mobilization which tore more than a million men from their homes and loved ones has been greeted with great jubilation. It was not in ignorance that the people showed such joy; they know the cost will be high. . . . It was patriotic fervor that inspired them to such manifestations. . . . Fully 90 percent of the population of Prague believe the city will be bombed at once . . . but they have swallowed their fear and reacted with enviable fortitude. . . .

A similar attitude prevailed throughout all of Czechoslovakia. In Bohemia and Moravia, in hundreds of towns and villages, youths reported for military duty and peasants supplied requisitioned horses, carts, and foodstuffs with pride and discipline; even in areas where Sudeten Nazi influence ran strong, mobilization orders were fully obeyed. Henlein's Free Corps men offered no resistance when they were rounded up by police and troops.

According to a British journalist, "The solidarity and unity of the Czech people was apparent on all sides. . . . From every cottage and farmhouse; from every school and public building, the Czech national flag flew. . . ."

On the evening of September 24, as the Czechoslovak Army dug in to defend the country, Chamberlain called a meeting of his cabinet and outlined what had taken place at Godesberg.

Duff Cooper, who believed the only way to handle Hitler was "to get tough," urged mobilization. Britain's military and naval leaders had already advised Chamberlain that it was "vital and important" to begin immediate mobilization, because "the realities of the situation indicate that we shall be at war with Germany in a few days' time."

When Chamberlain refused to concede this, Duff Cooper argued that at the least defensive measures to safeguard the Suez Canal should be taken, while Leslie Hore-Belisha, the secretary for war, recommended full mobilization of the Royal Navy and a callup of anti-aircraft and searchlight units as protection against a "sudden attack by the Luftwaffe."

But the Prime Minister, fearful that even such limited steps would offend Hitler and push him to war, categorically refused to take them. The meeting adjourned without decision as did one the following morning, Sunday, September 25.

Another cabinet meeting during the afternoon of the twenty-fifth produced nothing more than an attempt by Duff Cooper to resign. Only with difficulty did Chamberlain persuade the first lord of the admiralty to reconsider. It would have been disastrous for the Prime Minister if Duff Cooper had left the cabinet; his resignation might have toppled the Chamberlain government.

That afternoon, Jan Masaryk arrived at No. 10 Downing Street with the Czechoslovak answer to the Godesberg Memorandum. It was a flat turndown.

Masaryk told Chamberlain:

Against these new and cruel demands, my government feels bound to make their utmost resistance and we shall do so, with God's help. . . . The Czechoslovak nation . . . will not be a nation of slaves. . . . We rely upon the two great western democracies . . . to stand by us in our time of trial. . . .

Chamberlain brusquely dismissed Masaryk. Chamberlain's behavior moved the Czechoslovak ambassador to bewail to an aide the "calamity that this stupid and ill-informed man, a nonentity, should be the Prime Minister of Great Britain . . . at such a crucial moment. . . ."

Added to Prague's denunciation of the Godesberg Memorandum was that of the French. Daladier's cabinet, in an uncharacteristically militant display, not only rejected the memorandum, but also called for a partial mobilization. By early evening of the twenty-fifth, reservists were trooping to the colors. Shortly after adjourning, Daladier, accompanied by Bonnet and several aides, hurried through a driving rainstorm to Le Bourget Airport where they flew to London for an emergency conference with the British cabinet.

The French delegation reached No. 10 Downing Street at 9:25 P.M., September 25. After opening the session with a review of the Godesberg proceedings, Chamberlain called upon Daladier to present the French view.

"If after Austria, we allow the destruction of Czechoslovakia, what nation's turn will come next?" the French Premier asked. "If our two countries stand united against the rise of Nazism, stand against letting Hitler's program be carried through without a fight, would not other countries be encouraged to join us in this righteous struggle?"

Still seeking an alternative to war, Daladier suggested that an international commission be formed to arbitrate the whole Czechoslovakian question. This was an idea Hitler had already rejected, and Chamberlain was doubtful that the Fuehrer would change his mind now.

"Hitler is waiting for an answer of either yes or no. If it is no, he will invade Czechoslovakia at once. What will happen then?" Chamberlain asked.

"France will at once go to the aid of her ally," Daladier replied.

"And that will be war!" Chamberlain cried.

There followed an interrogation of Daladier by members of the British cabinet who opposed resistance. Only Duff Cooper and Hore-Belisha refrained from joining the examination of the French Premier. Question after question was hurled at Daladier about French military strength, tactics, strategy, supplies; so intense did the barrage of queries become that one witness termed it an "inquisition . . . not a quest for information. . . ."

Daladier's chief prosecutor was Sir John Simon, the chancellor of the exchequer, who kept up a "machine-gun" battery of inquiries. Did the French intend merely to man the Maginot Line or to

136

mount an offensive? Would the French Air Force be used against Germany or merely for defense? How exactly did the French intend to help the Czechoslovaks?

Daladier replied that strategic details did not interest him at this time. More important was France's moral obligations. He would not allow Hitler to destroy Czechoslovakia—to dominate Europe, and eventually the world.

Angry words were exchanged as the diplomats lost control of their emotions. "The discussion took on the aspects of a barroom brawl rather than a sober gathering of statesmen," a witness recalled.

Daladier stressed the "importance" of the Czechoslovak Army: a "well-equipped, well-officered force of nearly forty divisions." He appealed to his "British comrades of 1914–18, not to lose heart before the battle." French Army Intelligence believed that in spite of the "Germans having partly outflanked Czechoslovakian fortifications on the Austrian frontier . . . the Czechoslovaks could hold out alone against the Nazis for a month, perhaps longer, until massive help reached them. . . . And if the Russians came in, the combined Air Forces of Britain, France, and the Soviet Union could sweep the Luftwaffe from the skies. . . ."

This was the most optimistic appraisal of the military situation yet advanced by the French. But Daladier's euphoria did not convince the British. Chamberlain wanted to know still more about the French war plans. When the meeting broke up at 3:00 A.M., September 26, Chamberlain asked Daladier to summon General Gamelin by telephone for a meeting the next day, so that the Prime Minister might get a better picture of the French military condition.

Daladier complied and on Monday, September 26, General Gamelin arrived at Croydon in a downpour. He reached Downing Street shortly after 9:00 A.M. and went right in to see Chamberlain, accompanied by Daladier.

Significantly, Foreign Minister Georges Bonnet was excluded from the meeting and sent off to confer with Lord Halifax. Daladier did not want his colleague present because "Bonnet has a talent for discouraging everybody. . . . We need backbone, not chicanery. . . ."

The British government was reluctant to plunge into action with either their Air Force or Army. One cabinet member gloomily observed, "We're simply not ready. . . . We need time . . . and that's not all we have to worry about. What if we make an irrevocable move and the Poles jump on Czechoslovakia's back over the Teschen territory? We'll be in a pretty bag then, won't we?"

Shifting his position once again, General Gamelin presented Chamberlain with a rosy estimate of the military situation: France would have five million men mobilized, with about one hundred good divisions in the field at once. The Maginot Line permitted freedom of maneuver and almost certain security from a Nazi ground assault. While the French Air Force was inferior to the German, Gamelin assured Chamberlain that there were planes enough to give the Army a fair amount of air support and at the same time make it difficult for the Luftwaffe.

"France will suffer from air raids, but with firm belief in the justice of our cause, we shall hold fast until victory, no matter what hardships must be endured. When the first German bomb drops upon France, our nation will become welded in an unconquerable unity against the *boches*," Gamelin predicted.

As for the German Army, Gamelin had some disparaging comments to make. In the first place, he said, the German High Command was less than enthusiastic about waging a war at that time. He also indicated that French Intelligence had "wind of a plot" by a clique of generals to oust Hitler. The Siegfried Line was incomplete despite the best Nazi efforts. The Wehrmacht did not have sufficient supplies of many essential raw materials, especially oil, to conduct a long war. The greatest German advantage was the Luftwaffe—an undeniable menace to the Allies, but one which could be coped with, since "airpower alone is not decisive."

The Czechoslovaks, Gamelin believed, would fight well and possibly wreck Hitler's hopes of swift victory. Should Poland launch an invasion, the Czechoslovak difficulties would be greater, but not necessarily critical. "In my opinion," Gamelin said, "the Czechoslovak Army is capable of fighting on two fronts and will achieve stunning successes against the Poles."

After leaving Chamberlain, the French commander-in-chief addressed a gathering of top British Army, Navy, and Air Force officers. Gamelin repeated to them what he had told Chamberlain

138

and added information just received by cable. The Russian military attaché in Paris had pledged "thirty infantry divisions, a mass of cavalry, and many airplanes" to defend Czechoslovakia, should France honor her treaty.

Except for the Royal Navy officers present, none of the Britons at the meeting showed any inclination to fight; they were visibly unenthusiastic about the news of Russian support and unhappily mulled over the possibility that a Soviet-Polish war might break out if Stalin tried to send troops across Poland.

Gamelin made a poor impression on Britain's military leaders. One said of him, "his ideas are optimistic to the point of lunacy. . . ."

However, the British cabinet decided at 6:00 P.M., September 26, to declare a state of emergency. Orders for wartime mobilization went out to the Royal Navy; coastal defense units, antiaircraft groups, and searchlight detachments of the Territorial Army were called up. Great Britain was at last getting ready for war; seldom had any nation undertaken similar preparations with such reluctance.

But even as he initiated military measures, Chamberlain made one final effort to preserve peace. The Prime Minister dispatched Sir Horace Wilson to Berlin with a message calling upon Hitler to renounce the use of force, and suggesting instead, a Czechoslovak-German conference to settle peaceably the transfer of territory to the Reich. If requested, a British delegate would also sit on the commission.

In the event that Hitler would not agree to do this and insisted instead on the terms of the Godesberg Memorandum, Wilson was instructed to inform him that if German forces crossed the Czechoslovak frontier, French armies would attack Germany and "Great Britain would immediately enter the war on the side of France with all the military power at her command."

This was not the only "last attempt" for peace made on September 26. Warned by the U. S. ambassador to France, William C. Bullitt, and the U. S. ambassador to Great Britain, Joseph Kennedy (father of the late President John F. Kennedy), that war was only "days off, perhaps less," President Franklin D. Roosevelt sent a personal cablegram to Hitler, dispatching copies to

Benes, Chamberlain, Daladier, and the heads of other principal European countries.

Roosevelt's message was a plea for Hitler to avoid war in favor of negotiations. It said in part:

During the present crisis the people of the United States and their Government have earnestly hoped that the negotiations for the adjustment of the controversy which has now arisen in Europe might reach a successful conclusion. . . . So long as these negotiations continue . . . the world may escape the madness of a new resort to war. . . .

On behalf of the 130,000,000 people of the United States of America and for the sake of humanity everywhere, I most earnestly appeal to you not to break off negotiations looking to a peaceful, fair and constructive settlement of the questions at issue . . . so long as negotiations continue differences may be reconciled. Once they are broken off, reason is banished and force asserts itself . . . force produces no solution for the future good of humanity. . . .

Hitler made no response to this call for peace from the President of the United States. A high State Department official glumly told reporters, "The clouds have closed in over Europe. A fearful storm is about to break. . . . I believe the very foundations of the earth itself will be shaken before the sun breaks through again. . . . We are perched on the rim of disaster. . . ."

CHAPTER 19

Rain fell continuously all over western Europe and the British Isles on Monday, September 26; in Berlin, a windswept downpour pelted the German capital until some streets had ankle-deep puddles.

By 5:00 P.M., the rain had slackened and the weather gradually cleared.

At that hour, Chamberlain's special envoy, Sir Horace Wilson, together with Sir Neville Henderson and the interpreter, Ivone Kirkpatrick, left the British Embassy for the Chancellery where Hitler awaited them.

The Englishmen found the Fuehrer in a testy mood; ". . . he was nervous and jumpy . . . his cheeks were mottled, his brows furrowed . . . ," Kirkpatrick recalled.

Wilson and his companions knew that Hitler was to address a huge Nazi rally at the Berlin *Sportspalast* a few hours later. They believed that the Fuehrer's tenseness had to do with his forthcoming speech.

After perfunctory greetings, Hitler indicated that the meeting should get down to its business. Wilson handed to Schmidt the message from Chamberlain, and the interpreter started to translate it aloud for the Fuehrer.

"The Czechoslovakian government [Chamberlain had written] informs me that . . . they regard as wholly unacceptable the proposal in your Memorandum for the immediate evacuation of the areas and their immediate occupation by German troops. . . ."

Schmidt got no farther. With a strangled cry, Hitler jumped to

141

his feet and stamped angrily for the door shrieking, "There's no point at all in going on with these negotiations!"

Wilson, quite upset, begged the Fuehrer to hear the rest of the letter. His wrath poorly concealed, Hitler flopped back into a chair, gnawing at his lips, jaw muscles working, glaring at everyone in the room. He grunted permission for Schmidt to continue.

The interpreter went on, and Hitler listened in brooding silence until Schmidt read:

In communicating with me about your proposals, the government of Czechoslovakia point out that they . . . would be deprived of every safeguard for national existence. Czechoslovakia would have to yield up large proportions of her carefully prepared defenses and admit the German Armies deep into her territory. . . . Her national and economic independence would automatically disappear with the acceptance of the German plan. . . .

At these words, Hitler leaped up again, his features contorted in rage, and charged about the room, shouting incoherently. Schmidt remembered later, "For the first time in my presence, Hitler completely lost his head."

The Fuehrer cursed Benes, the Czechoslovaks, Chamberlain, Wilson, and the world at large. Shaking his fists, he screamed, "On October first I shall have Czechoslovakia where I want her. If France and England decide to strike, let them. I don't care a *pfennig!*"

Somehow, Wilson managed to calm him down so that the talks could proceed. The Fuehrer finally put an end to the meeting. "Tell your Czech friends to have someone in Berlin who is prepared to accept the Godesberg Memorandum. They have until two o'clock in the afternoon of September 28! Tell them that's my last word!"

Confused and shaken by Hitler's outbursts, Wilson took his leave, reminding the Fuehrer that he and his colleagues would remain in Berlin overnight and asking for another audience in the morning. Hitler grudgingly granted the request.

The tantrum Hitler had thrown during his meeting with the British delegation was merely a warmup for the performance he put on at the Berlin *Sportspalast* that night before twenty thousand howling, flag-waving Nazis.

Hitler's speech was delivered in "absolute fury," according to the American reporter, William L. Shirer. The Nazi chieftain raved and blustered. His venomous insults of President Benes boiled out at "gutter level." Seldom, if ever, had the head of a modern nation resorted to public use of such untrammeled vulgarity.

The Fuehrer's followers responded to every threat, every boast, every insult with frenzied cries of *"Heil Hitler!"* and *"Seig heil!"* Hitler vowed to have the Sudetenland by October 1, no matter what obstacles were placed in his way. Again, he assured Chamberlain that once the Sudeten problem was solved, he would want nothing more for Germany in Europe. "We want no Czechs!" Hitler yelled. "My patience is ended . . . the patience of the German people is ended! War or peace! We shall gain what is rightfully ours! Let Benes choose! Germany is ready to stand against the world if necessary!"

When the Fuehrer had finished, Joseph Goebbels, who had been seated next to him, jumped up to the microphones and cried, "One thing is sure: 1918 will never be repeated!"

At this, Hitler shot out of his chair, "a maniacal expression on his face," an eyewitness noted, and with all the power of his lungs bellowed, *"Ja!"* As if this effort were too much, the Fuehrer tottered to his chair and collapsed in it, "like a monstrous marionette, suddenly unstrung. . . ."

The *Sportspalast* speech sent a shudder of apprehension around the globe. Prime Minister Chamberlain responded to Hitler's hour-and-a-half harangue with a statement broadcast after midnight. Britons who were still awake heard their Prime Minister's quavering voice pleading with Hitler not to resort to war:

It seems to me incredible that the peoples of Europe who do not want war . . . should be plunged into a bloody struggle over a question in which agreement has already been largely obtained. It is evident that Chancellor Hitler has no faith that the promises made will be carried out. . . . Speaking for the British government, we regard ourselves morally responsible for seeing that the

143

promises are carried out . . . with all reasonable promptitude
provided that the German government will agree to the settle-
ment . . . by discussion and not by force.
I trust that Chancellor Hitler will not reject this proposal . . .
if accepted . . . it will satisfy the German desire for the union of
the Sudeten Germans with the Reich without the shedding of blood
in any part of Europe. . . .

On Tuesday, September 27, at noon, Sir Horace Wilson went
back to see Hitler. If possible, the German leader was in an even
worse mood than the day before. A rather inept diplomat, Wilson
clumsily tried to placate the Fuehrer with complimentary remarks
about Hitler's *Sportspalast* speech. He also reminded the Fuehrer
of Chamberlain's statement. Did Herr Hitler have any message
for the British Prime Minister?

"No!" Hitler announced. "There is nothing more to say! Prague
can either accept or reject my terms. If they turn me down tell your
Prime Minister that I will smash the Czechs! I will bomb Prague!
I will decimate the Czech Army! I will make Benes run like the
criminal he is!"

Pale and tense, Wilson said, "I must now remind you, Herr
Hitler, that if France, in fulfillment of her treaty obligations,
should become engaged in hostilities with Germany, my country
would be obliged to support France. . . ."

"I can only take note of your position," Hitler replied angrily.
"It means that if France elects to attack Germany, England will
feel obliged to attack her also! All right! Today is Tuesday, we
shall be at war next Monday! The Czechs, feeling supported, will
reject my note! Good! I shall destroy Czechoslovakia!"

"I did not say France would attack Germany," Wilson responded.

"It makes no difference to me if France and England strike.
Let them do so! I have spent millions on my fortifications in the
west! They can attack when they like!" Hitler declared.

Wilson wanted to go on with this pointless exchange, but Henderson nudged him and whispered that it was time to leave. On the
way out, Wilson managed a few words aside with Hitler. "I shall
try to make these Czechs sensible," Wilson promised.

Hitler nodded. *"Ja!* I would welcome that. But remember, if war comes, I will not attack France. Should you invade us, then the aggression will be yours."

When Chamberlain learned this, his reluctance to enter a war grew even stronger. If the Germans remained on the defensive in the west, the British and French position was weakened. The Allies had expected something else: massive bombings of London and Paris; a powerful German assault on the Maginot Line. Under such circumstances, an offensive against Germany was justified. But with the Germans remaining on the defensive, Britain and France would have to wage aggressive warfare—a role for which Chamberlain and Daladier had no stomach.

But shortly after Wilson, Henderson, and Kirkpatrick had left, Hitler ordered the first assault units of Case Green to take up their positions. The invasion hour was tentatively set for 6:15 A.M., October 1. Later the same day, Hitler transferred five regular divisions to duty in the west as reinforcements for the nine German divisions, frontier guards, and labor battalions already holding the Siegfried Line.

It was no accident that churches in almost every European city were crowded with worshipers that Wednesday. An air of imminent disaster hung over London, Paris, Berlin, and Prague.

In the British capital unemployed men dug trenches in public parks; anti-aircraft units of the Territorial Army set up their guns at strategic points around London.

Young men in RAF uniforms hurried to railroad depots to entrain for their flying fields. On motion picture screens in London theaters notices flashed reminding parents to have their children fitted for gas masks at the nearest police station.

But in spite of the war menace, London somehow seemed gayer; gallows humor abounded, wry jokes about the beneficial effect of bombing: "Won't be any slums left in London when old Adolf gets through," people said. "They'll be knocked flat."

In Czechoslovakia, Jews and anti-Nazis fled from the Sudeten areas leaving behind homes, businesses, and personal belongings. There was no time to pack, to sell; all that mattered was to get out before the Germans came. No trains ran to Germany, and Czechoslovak military engineers began blowing up bridges to hinder the impending Nazi advance.

145

More than one million men were under arms in France, and that number grew hourly. Observers who had seen the French go to war in 1914 and remembered the cheering crowds, the flowers strewn before the soldiers, the kisses, the flag-waving, the bands playing *"La Marseillaise"* was shocked at the dispirited attitudes of the *poilus*—the ordinary French soldier.

Gone was the famous *élan* and *esprit;* reserve regiments "plodded down the boulevards like cattle shambling to slaughter; there were no bands, no songs, no cheers, only sobbing and the shuffling feet of marching men," an American reporter wrote.

As the troops moved eastward, masses of refugees trudged away from the border in sad-faced groups, carrying bundles and pushing baby carriages laden with household belongings.

To prevent German spies from attempting to communicate with Berlin via carrier pigeon, military authorities ordered all such birds destroyed. In frontier villages, piles of feathered pigeon corpses mounted in the squares.

If all hope for peace seemed lost, Chamberlain had not yet given up his cherished dream of being memorialized as a peacemaker. When Sir Horace Wilson returned with the dismal report of failure, Chamberlain began bombarding President Benes with a series of telegrams, urging the Czechoslovak leader to yield before the deadline at 2:00 P.M., September 28.

The British Minister had new proposals, none of which offered the Czechoslovaks more security than did the Godesberg Memorandum; Chamberlain merely suggested that Czechoslovakia be given a stay of execution from October 1 to October 10 so that an international commission might be set up to oversee the transfer of the Sudetenland. No guarantees were offered the Czechoslovaks for their future independence. Benes could not accept such terms, even if it meant sparing his country the horrors of war.

Bonnet had another idea. If Germany invaded Czechoslovakia, the French would refrain from taking offensive action against the Nazis; in a short time Czechoslovakia would be overrun, Hitler would be satisfied, and a deal could be made to end the danger of a major war. He mentioned this to Daladier, whose only response, according to an eyewitness, was "an icy glare."

Meanwhile, Hitler began having a few second thoughts. During

146

the course of Tuesday, September 27, he received yet another message from Roosevelt urging him not to take the fatal step.

The American President wrote:

The present negotiations still stand open. They can be continued if you give the word. Should the need for supplementing them become evident, nothing stands in the way of widening their scope into a conference of all nations directly interested in the present controversy. . . .

FDR also ordered the U. S. ambassador in Rome to deliver a confidential message to Il Duce from the President of the United States. Roosevelt asked Mussolini's help to "continue the present peace efforts . . . to reach an agreement on the questions still outstanding . . . by peaceful means rather than by turning to force. . . ."

The King of Sweden advised Hitler that unless Germany extended indefinitely his time limit of September 28, world war would inevitably break out. Germany would be solely to blame for it and inevitably would lose it "in view of the present combination of Powers."

Other information of a sobering nature reached Hitler. A dispatch from Budapest informed him that Yugoslavia and Rumania had warned the Hungarian government that they would move against Hungary if she attacked Czechoslovakia. This would spread the war to the Balkans, an eventuality that Hitler did not want.

Moreover, the German military attaché in Paris notified Berlin that the French partial mobilization so resembled a total one "that I foresee the deployment of sixty-five first-class divisions on the German frontier by the sixth day of mobilization. . . ." (Germany, at best, would have fourteen divisions on that front, several of them barely trained reserve troops.) The attaché also reported that three hundred RAF planes had landed on French airfields, although this was not fully confirmed as yet. From London came word that the Royal Navy had gone on a war footing "in remarkably swift time."

It was learned that Mussolini was talking about mobilizing; but Il Duce had no intention of sending his troops to the French border. Instead, they would be concentrated in Libya, which was no help to Hitler.

The Fuehrer's Italian ally wanted to avoid a major conflict despite his pledge to march with Hitler against the "decadent democracies." No one knew better than Mussolini that the Italian Army, Navy, and Air Force were not in shape for full-scale war.

As if these jolts were not enough, Generalissimo Francisco Franco, the Spanish leader, who owed everything to Hitler and Mussolini, made a startling about-face. He announced his intentions of declaring his neutrality in any conflict beyond the Spanish border and was already making certain that none of the German or Italian forces in Spain were allowed within 150 kilometers of the French frontier.

Franco, still deeply involved in the civil war he had started, was not going to commit himself; the Spanish rebel had no desire to back Hitler if Germany ran the slightest risk of losing. Evidently Franco believed this to be more than a possibility.

The Fuehrer received yet another unpleasant surprise, this time from a completely unexpected source. Propaganda Minister Goebbels advised Hitler that, with war looming, the German public should be "galvanized and stirred"; the canny Goebbels proposed a parade to "whip up" the people. Hitler then ordered a crack motorized division to pass through Berlin at 5:00 P.M., just at the time when offices and factories would be closing and the capital's streets jammed with homebound workers.

The show was a flop.

The British ambassador, Sir Neville Henderson, watched the display of armor and noted: "It is well known how much Germans love military displays . . . but not a single individual applauded its passage. The picture which it represented was that of a hostile army traversing a conquered city. . . . Perhaps at that moment Hitler realized . . . that the cheers of fanatics in the *Sportspalast* did not express the true feelings of the German people. . . ."

American correspondent William L. Shirer recorded the scene in his diary:

I went out to the corner of the Linden where the column of troops was turning down the Wilhelmstrasse, expecting to see a tremendous demonstration. . . . I had read of 1914 when cheer-

148

*ing throngs on this same street tossed flowers at the marching sol-
diers and the girls ran up and kissed them. . . . But today they
ducked into subways, refused to look on, and the handful that did,
stood at the curb in utter silence. . . . It was the most striking
demonstration against war I've ever seen. . . .*

Later, Shirer went along the Wilhelmstrasse to the Chancellery
building where Hitler was reviewing the troops from a balcony.
He observed:

*There weren't two hundred people there. Hitler looked grim,
then angry and soon went inside, leaving his troops to pass by un-
reviewed. . . . What I've seen tonight almost rekindles a little
faith in the German people. . . . They're dead set against
war. . . .*

On the eve of the expiration of his ultimatum, 2:00 P.M., September 28, the Fuehrer knew definitely that the French Army was
mobilizing, that the British Navy was on a war footing, and that
Prague was boldly defiant.

Whether for propaganda purposes or other reasons, Hitler
called in Schmidt and dictated to him a letter for Chamberlain.
The Fuehrer's note was mild, lacking the bluster and bombast he
had previously displayed. From its tone, Schmidt felt, "the Fuehrer is shrinking from war."

In the letter Hitler denied that he intended to "rob Czechoslovakia of every guarantee of its existence" or that his troops would
advance further than agreed upon. He was prepared to discuss
with the Czechoslovaks the details of the occupation and to "give
a formal guarantee for the remainder of Czechoslovakia." It must
be clear to reasonable men, Hitler said, that the Czechoslovaks
were holding out simply because they hoped, with the help of Eng
land and France, to bring on a war. Even now, Hitler declared, he
did not want to "slam the door on peace."

In conclusion, the Fuehrer said, "I must leave it to your judgment whether, in view of this, you consider that you should continue your efforts . . . to bring the Prague government to its senses
at the very last hour. . . ."

CHAPTER 20

In both London and Paris, September 27 had been a busy day. The French government was disunited; Daladier was ready to fight one moment and to give in the next. Bonnet maneuvered frantically to find a way for France to evade her responsibility toward Czechoslovakia.

Paul Reynaud, on the other hand, called for "war to the death" against the menace of Hitlerism. Communists and anti-Nazis held riotous demonstrations, demanding a popular front against the Germans.

The French ambassador in Berlin, André François-Poncet, on instructions from Bonnet, informed Hitler that the foreign minister would work until the last possible second to convince the Czechoslovaks that war against Germany was suicidal. Hitler had no need to fight, François-Poncet argued; all the Fuehrer's essential demands had been met. If he held back his armies, the French Foreign Office would "force" Benes to evacuate the Sudetenland by October 1.

Prime Minister Chamberlain also applied pressure on the Czechoslovaks. In a note to Benes, he warned that the German Army would receive orders to cross the Czechoslovak frontier unless Prague accepted the German conditions.

He further warned that "Bohemia would be overrun by the Wehrmacht and nothing which another Power or Powers could do would be able to save your country and your people from such a fate. This remains true whatever the results of a world war might be."

The question of war or peace was not up to Hitler, but to Benes,

Chamberlain maintained. He refused to assume the responsibility of telling the Czechoslovaks what to do, however. It was their decision.

This message was followed by another in which Chamberlain suggested to Benes that the Czechoslovaks allow the Germans a limited military occupation on October 1—outside the fortification line. Then, a German-Czechoslovak-British commission would establish the remainder of the areas to be ceded to Germany. (This proposal was passed on to Hitler as well.) The only alternative, Chamberlain said, "was invasion and dismemberment for Czechoslovakia." The country could not be reconstituted along the old borders "no matter what the outcome of a conflict, with its incalculable loss of life and property, might be."

In short, the Prime Minister was telling Benes that even if Germany were defeated, the Sudetenland would be lost. The meaning was clear: there was no point in fighting for something that could never be regained. France, Chamberlain pointed out, concurred in this opinion.

Having done what he could to discourage the Czechoslovaks and undermine their determination to resist, Chamberlain broadcast a speech to the British people. It was probably the strangest talk ever delivered by a national leader who was supposed to be rallying his country for war. From his first sentence, Chamberlain set a melancholy note:

How horrible, how fantastic, how incredible it is that we should be digging trenches and trying on gas masks because of a quarrel in a faraway country between people of whom we know nothing. It seems all the more impossible that a quarrel which has already been settled in principle should be the subject of war. . . .

Hitler . . . told me privately, and he publicly repeated it yesterday evening, that once the Sudeten German incident was settled that would be the end of German territorial claims in Europe.

I shall not give up hope nor abandon my efforts to maintain the peace so long as there is a chance of success. I would not hesitate to pay even a third visit to Germany if I thought it would do any good. But at present I do not see that I can usefully do any more in the field of mediation. . . .

Chamberlain's speech had the effect of "throwing a wet blanket on a smoldering fire," an English journalist wrote. "A few more speeches like that and we'll all go out and slit our throats," a Laborite member of Parliament remarked. "I don't know who old Neville was trying to encourage—us or the Jerries," a working-class listener snorted.

In spite of the Prime Minister's spiritless talk, the British nation continued to prepare for war. Fleet mobilization was increased; RAF fighters and bombers waited armed and ready on military flying fields; special trains began evacuating schoolchildren from the crowded districts of London. That night most Britons went to bed in the belief that the next day might see them at war.

A special courier reached No. 10 Downing Street with Hitler's letter to Chamberlain at 10:30 P.M. The Prime Minister read the note eagerly and promptly answered:

After reading your letter, I feel certain that you can get all essentials without war, and without delay. I am ready to come to Berlin myself at once to discuss arrangements with you . . . together with representatives of France and Italy. . . . I cannot believe that you will take the responsibility of starting a world war . . . for the sake of a few days delay in settling this long-standing problem. . . .

Chamberlain also dispatched a telegram to Mussolini asking him to persuade Hitler to accept the plan and to attend the proposed meeting.

The Prime Minister's message to Il Duce had its desired effect. On Wednesday, September 28, at 10:00 A.M., Lord Perth, the British ambassador to Rome, called on Italy's foreign minister, Count Galeazzo Ciano, Mussolini's son-in-law, telling him that only the Duce could salvage peace. Mussolini must persuade Hitler to refrain from any warlike action. Britain and France, Perth stressed, were ready to fight, and a European conflict was sure to break out unless Hitler stayed his invasion of Czechoslovakia.

"There is no time to be lost," Ciano cried. "It is a question of hours; not days!" The Italian foreign minister then dashed off to confer with his father-in-law. An hour later, Mussolini was on the telephone talking to Bernardo Attolico, his ambassador in Berlin. He instructed Attolico to request an audience with Hitler at once. "Tell him the British have asked me . . . to mediate the Sudeten question. The point of difference is very small. Tell him to hold up any action for twenty-four hours. Tell the Fuehrer that Fascist Italy is solidly behind him. *I* am behind him! He must decide! But tell him that I favor accepting the suggestion. Do you hear?"

"*Si,* Duce, I hear," Attolico said.

"Then hurry! The time is running out!"

As Attolico headed for the Chancellory building, Hitler was receiving the French ambassador, André François-Poncet. The Frenchman noticed the tension that "vibrated throughout the Chancellory. . . . Officers looking grim and nervous rushed about. . . . There were whispered conferences and worried frowns, as generals, colonels, and other high-ranking military men stamped in and out of the place. . . . Hitler was in the midst of the confusion, wandering rather aimlessly, stopping to talk now and then to an aide or to an official such as Von Ribbentrop, Goering, or General Keitel. . . ."

At 11:45 A.M., Hitler motioned François-Poncet into a conference room. Von Ribbentrop was present and also Paul Schmidt, whose abilities as an interpreter were not needed because François-Poncet spoke fluent German.

The ambassador tried to reason with Hitler. "Do not think, Herr Chancellor, that you can confine the conflict to Czechoslovakia. If you attack, you will set all Europe afire. You are convinced, of course, that you will win, just as we are convinced that we shall. But why do you want to run an enormous risk when you can satisfy your claims without war?" François-Poncet argued.

His words brought on a Hitler tantrum; the Fuehrer shrieked, cursed, and vowed to wipe out the "mongrel Czechs." However, his performance did not rattle the suave Frenchman, who waited for the storm to pass and then repeated that Hitler could have everything he wanted without a war in which Germany might well be defeated.

When Von Ribbentrop interrupted with the boast that Germany could smash any combination of powers, François-Poncet said icily, "I am speaking to the Chancellor, not you, Herr von Ribbentrop. When I want your opinion, I'll ask for it!"

154

Hitler chuckled over Von Ribbentrop's obvious discomfit and, in a better mood, gave François-Poncet permission to proceed. The ambassador unfolded a French proposal, dreamed up by Bonnet, to placate the Nazis. Bonnet was determined to go Chamberlain one better; where the British Prime Minister offered Hitler the occupation by October 1 of only a tiny enclave in the Sudetenland, the French foreign minister proposed to hand over almost the entire Sudeten region on the same date. Bonnet suggested that French troops be rushed into the Sudetenland to maintain order until all negotiations were settled.

Before Hitler made any response, an aide entered to tell the Fuehrer that Attolico was outside with a message from Mussolini. Hitler terminated his interview with François-Poncet, promising to answer the French proposal that afternoon. The ambassador left, puzzling over this abrupt dismissal. He was ushered out a rear door and Hitler, accompanied by Schmidt, hurried to attend Attolico.

The Italian ambassador, quite distraught, was pacing about an antechamber. In the half-hour since Mussolini's phone call, Attolico had run into nerve-wracking delays while trying to reach Hitler. Neither the Embassy car nor his chauffeur could be located to drive him to the Chancellory. After much shouting and arm-waving he found a taxicab, only to be stalled in traffic. By the time Attolico reached the Chancellory, he was "red-faced and panting," according to Schmidt.

When he spotted Hitler, the Italian cried from some distance away, "Fuehrer! I have an urgent communication for you from the Duce!" Aided by Schmidt, Attolico, who spoke scarcely any German, told Hitler about Mussolini's offer of mediation, not concealing the fact that it stemmed from the British. All that was asked of Germany was to refrain from taking action for another day. Mussolini would telephone at noon for the Fuehrer's answer. It was then 11:50 A.M., only two hours before the expiration of the German ultimatum.

Hitler paused for a moment to consider the request. Then, drawing a deep breath, he said, "Tell the Duce that I accept his proposal!"

Attolico could not hide his pleasure; his eyes sparkled behind his thick-lensed glasses. "Thank you, Fuehrer. Remember, no

155

matter what happens, the Duce vows that Italy will stand behind you!" He then hurried off to his Embassy to pass the word back to Rome.

(Since Case Green was scheduled to start at 6:15 A.M., October 1, Hitler had actually postponed nothing; his acceptance of an apparent postponement was pure propaganda, to make him seem a proponent of peace.)

After further negotiations, including a talk with Sir Neville Henderson and a second meeting with François-Poncet, Hitler agreed to the proposed conference. He imposed certain conditions, however. In the first place, Hitler refused to meet with Benes or any other representative of the Czechoslovak government.

Further, the conference must be limited to four powers—France, England, Germany, and Italy. No other country, particularly not the Soviet Union, could be included under any circumstances.

Another condition was that Mussolini should be present in person. Here, Hitler was appealing to the Duce's vanity. He knew Mussolini would be pleased by such a token of Axis solidarity.

Lastly, the conference must take place on German soil, thus making the Nazis appear masters of the situation. It would be Chamberlain's third trip to Germany and Daladier's first; to the world it would seem that they were coming as supplicants. Hitler also insisted that only Germany send invitations to the conference.

All these points were settled, in turn, to Hitler's satisfaction after four more visits from Attolico in under three hours, and twenty telephone calls between Berlin and Rome. (Mussolini later gave a two-thousand-lire tip to the operator who had handled the telephone calls.)

The scene was set for the great betrayal.

CHAPTER 21

While Hitler and Mussolini were involved in one of history's longest and most expensive telephone marathons, the British House of Commons met to hear Prime Minister Chamberlain report on the international situation.

Every member capable of being present was in the packed House; the galleries were as crowded as "the underground in rush hour." Among the distinguished visitors were Queen Mary and such peers of the realm as Lord Halifax and former Prime Minister Stanley Baldwin, now elevated to the rank of earl. The diplomatic section was filled with representatives of many countries. Seated in a front row was Jan Masaryk of Czechoslovakia.

Prime Minister Chamberlain, rising to speak at 2:55 P.M., was greeted by cries of "Hear! Hear!" from his supporters. Standing stiffly, a heavy gold watch chain slung across his vest, wearing an old-fashioned celluloid collar and a broad black tie, Chamberlain looked more like a professor of ancient history than the leader of an empire.

He reminded one newsman of "my patrician uncle who would not permit any flicker of emotion to cross his face; the sort of man who could stub a bare toe without grimacing."

Chamberlain gave a dry recital of recent events. From time to time, he was interrupted by applause, which became particularly fervent when he made it quite plain that he was still more interested in preserving peace than in saving Czechoslovakia. After he had been speaking for an hour and twenty minutes, the audience began to grow restless; it was now 4:15 P.M., and his listeners hoped the speech was nearing its end.

157

Chamberlain was saying, "Whatever view honorable members may have had about Signor Mussolini, I think that they will appreciate the service he has just rendered in the cause of peace. . . . Through the Duce's good offices, Herr Hitler has agreed to delay German action for twenty-four hours. . . ."

This brought a burst of hand-clapping and as the speaker paused, Sir John Simon, chancellor of the exchequer, who for several minutes had been trying to catch Chamberlain's attention, gave him a note that had been passed down from the peers' gallery by Lord Halifax.

Chamberlain glanced at the paper and a radiant expression crossed his normally austere face. Holding a hand up for silence, he said, in a strained voice, "That is not all. I have something further to say to the House yet. I have now been informed by Herr Hitler that he invites me to meet him at Munich tomorrow morning. He has also invited Signor Mussolini and Monsieur Daladier. Signor Mussolini has accepted and I have no doubt that Monsieur Daladier will accept. I need not say what my answer will be. . . ."

This brought the House to its feet; members climbed atop benches, shouted, cheered, pounded one another on the back, threw hats and briefcases in the air. Cascades of papers fell like giant snowflakes. In the visitors' gallery Queen Mary sobbed without restraint. Never before had the august House of Commons known such sights.

Winston Churchill did not join the emotional demonstration. He slouched in his seat, calling out to his exuberant colleagues, "And what about the Czechs? Does no one care about their opinion?"

One man present did. Jan Masaryk, in the diplomatic gallery, covered his face with his hands and wept. Later, he went to No. 10 Downing Street to see Chamberlain and Halifax and asked whether Czechoslovakia would be invited to Munich. Somewhat abashed, Chamberlain explained that it would not; Hitler had made it clear that the conference was off if the Czechoslovaks attended.

Masaryk stared with distaste at the British statesmen. "Very well, gentlemen," he said. "So be it. If you destroy my country to preserve the peace of the world, I will be the first to applaud you. But if not, may God help your souls!"

158

Before evening, Daladier announced that he would be in Munich, to the disgust of a few and the delight of most Frenchmen. The news of the Munich Conference reached Prague at about 6:00 P.M. Benes immediately telephoned Chamberlain and was assured that the British Prime Minister intended to keep "the interests of Czechoslovakia fully in mind."

In Moscow, there was anger and irritation over Munich. Stalin had wanted the Czechoslovak dispute settled through a general conference with the Soviet Union participating. Now, the powers were acting as though Russian opinion on the Czechoslovak crisis did not matter.

The Munich Conference ended any further discussion by the Wehrmacht "conspirators" of ousting Hitler. The meeting lessened the threat of war, and the opportunity was lost. Most historians seriously doubt that there had ever been any danger to the Fuehrer from his generals. In September 1939, the same "rebels" willingly followed Hitler into war. Not until Germany was near defeat in 1944 did the military offer any threat to the Fuehrer.

Through the years there has been much speculation among historians about Hitler's reasons for agreeing to the Munich meeting. Some believe he was influenced by his lack of military allies—Mussolini dreaded the outbreak of a general war, Hungary would not march, no other country except Hitler's Germany wanted war. Some feel that British and French military preparations caused Hitler to reconsider attacking Czechoslovakia.

Among other theories advanced was that Hitler feared a revolt by generals reluctant to engage in a conflict with France, Britain, and possibly Russia. Also, there were symptoms of apathy toward the impending war among the German people. All these factors may have helped to bring Hitler to the conference table, but the main motivation was the Fuehrer's realization that he could have everything he wanted without resorting to war.

The principal actors in the drama that was to take place in Munich started for the scene at different times. Mussolini left Rome by special train at 6:30 P.M., September 28. He was accompanied by Count Ciano and a group of Fascist luminaries. The Black Shirts were in high spirits; the conference at Munich offered Italy a chance to assume a major role in European events. Mussolini relished playing the peacemaker. As a warrior he had not fared

159

too well. Now, riding in his luxurious train, surrounded by satraps, he was well pleased with himself.

Mussolini's train reached Kufstein, an Austrian town on the Italian border, at 9:30 A.M. There it was boarded by Hitler, Von Ribbentrop and a covey of generals. The two dictators embraced warmly. The Fuehrer seemed in an agitated mood; he talked compulsively about "settling accounts" with France, outlining to Il Duce German strategy on the western front in the war that was to come.

"We shall fight side by side against France and England," Hitler predicted. "It is just as well, Duce, that it will happen while we both are young and vigorous. . . ."

As the train clacked off the miles to Munich, Hitler ranted on and on against the democracies, repeating all the familiar clichés about the Versailles Treaty, the humiliation of Germany, and the traitors of 1918. Mussolini listened patiently, from time to time interjecting a thought of his own on the subject.

But when the train approached Munich, Il Duce cut in to ask about the upcoming conference. With evident relief, Von Ribbentrop handed him a memorandum that had been drawn up in the German Foreign Office. The paper contained the demands to be presented at the conference; Il Duce was to make it appear that he had formulated them as a basis for mediation.

The Italian leader studied the proposals and nodded in agreement. He then settled back as Hitler resumed his tirade.

At Munich, Hitler and Mussolini proceeded in an open limousine through heiling crowds, past smartly uniformed soldiers at stiff attention, toward the Fuehrerhaus where the conference was to be held.

Premier Daladier took off from Le Bourget Airfield at 8:45 A.M., Thursday, September 29, in an Air France twin-motored plane named *Poitu*. The weather was not auspicious for the trip; a milk-white fog enshrouded the environs of Paris.

Members of the cabinet and a crowd of several hundred Parisians gathered at Le Bourget to bid the Premier farewell. An honor guard of air cadets snappily presented arms as Daladier's car rolled up; somewhere, nearby, muffled by the fog, a band played march music.

The onlookers, who could barely make out the *Poitu* waiting on the runway, cheered *"Vive* Daladier!" and *"Vive la paix!"* The Premier, wearing a dark suit, dark overcoat, and dark felt hat, waved through the fog at his supporters. Members of his staff hurried up the steps into the aircraft and Daladier followed, pausing at the top for a final wave. "Never once did he smile," an eyewitness recalled. "In his dark clothing, and with his dour expression, he reminded me of a funeral director. . . ."

The *Poitu* rolled out onto the runway and, gathering speed, roared into the fog. Spectators peered through the damp haze trying to catch a glimpse of the departing plane, wondering if it was properly airborne. Overhead, motors droned and throbbed; a ragged cheer arose, and the crowd slowly scattered.

The big day started early for Prime Minister Neville Chamberlain. He rose at 6:00 A.M. and by 7:30 A.M. left No. 10 Downing Street, bidding Mrs. Chamberlain goodbye on the doorstep. As his car headed for Croydon, Chamberlain was hailed by many thousands of Londoners who gathered along the way.

At the airfield, every member of the cabinet was present, as well as a large crowd of onlookers. Journalists, newsreel cameramen, photographers, radio broadcasters, and technicians formed a sizable group assembled to cover the historic departure.

Shortly before takeoff, as a light rain fell, Chamberlain stood before the radio microphones and delivered a short statement. "When I was a little boy," he said, "I used to repeat, 'If at first you don't succeed, try, try, try again.' This is what I am doing. When I come back I hope I may be able to say, as Hotspur says in Shakespeare's *Henry IV,* 'Out of this nettle, danger, we pluck this flower, safety.'"

Promptly at 8:35 A.M., Mr. Chamberlain and his aides—Sir William Strang, Sir Horace Wilson, Sir William Malkin, and Mr. Frank T. A. Ashton-Gwatkin—boarded their aircraft and took off. A wildly enthusiastic demonstration erupted as the plane rose higher in the sky and disappeared toward the east.

Chamberlain's Electra set down at Oberweisenfeld at 11:05 A.M. There Nazi dignitaries greeted the British delegation and escorted them to the sumptuous Hotel Regina, through streets bedecked with German, French, English, and Italian flags. For the third time, Chamberlain was waved, cheered, and heiled by crowds of Germans.

161

Daladier received a no less enthusiastic ovation when he landed at 11:15 A.M. His headquarters was another splendid hotel, the Vier Jahreszeiten, where he arrived shortly before noon.

Unlike Hitler and Mussolini, the British and French had not consulted with each other that morning. Apparently neither Daladier at the Vier Jahreszeiten, nor Chamberlain at the Regina, deemed it necessary to meet before the conference to establish a joint program of action. The Allies seemed bound only by a mutual desire to appease Hitler.

The outcome of the Munich Conference was decided before it began.

CHAPTER 22

The site of the conference, the Fuehrerhaus, was a huge palace built by the Nazis. Its lines were Greek, its proportions German—a massive and rigid structure with wide corridors, marble staircases, reception rooms, thick red carpeting, vast fireplaces, and deep armchairs. One observer called it a "monument to bad taste."

At noon, the French and British delegations started for the Fuehrerhaus. To an eyewitness it appeared that the entire population of Munich "had turned out to watch the dignitaries arrive at the conference site." The cheering crowds gave the old city the air of a holiday rather than a solemn occasion on which the fate of Europe hinged.

For such an important conference, the arrangements were slipshod. There was neither an agenda nor even any ink in the inkwells. According to one British reporter, the huge room in which the meeting was held "had the atmosphere of an execution chamber where sat a kangaroo court."

The attitudes of the principals provided sharp contrasts: Mussolini beamed effusively; Chamberlain was sober and serious; Hitler looked angry; Daladier was quiet and moody. The French Premier seemed "on the verge of vomiting," an observer recalled.

At twelve forty-five, the meeting started with a furious harangue by Hitler. Some of the sting was taken out of his vituperation during the translation by Schmidt into English and French for the benefit of Daladier and Chamberlain. (Mussolini was fluent in German, English, and French.)

Hitler's opening remarks did not bode well for the success of the meeting. "The existence of Czechoslovakia in her present

163

form," he said, "is a danger for the peace of Europe. . . . The Hungarian, Polish, and Russo-Carpathian minorities, incorporated by force into the Czechoslovak state, are revolting against the continuance of that state."

Of course, the Fuehrer admitted, he could speak only for the German minority, which he proceeded to do, recounting once again the "sufferings" of the Sudetenlanders, whom he was sworn to rescue from the clutches of the "vicious and sadistic Czechs."

"I have agreed to refrain from direct action only for a period of twenty-four hours out of friendship for Mussolini," Hitler continued. "In my speech at the *Sportspalast,* I stated that whatever happened, I should enter Czechoslovakia by October 1. The objection was raised that this act would have a violent character. . . . Very well, let us take advantage of the fact that we are gathered together to remove this character from it! But it must be done quickly! With a little good will it ought to be possible to evacuate the territories within ten days, perhaps even within six or seven. . . ."

Hitler's threatening tone roused Daladier to state, "I should like the Chancellor to make his intentions clear. If, as I have understood him, he means to destroy Czechoslovakia as an independent state and purely and simply . . . to annex it . . . I know what remains for me to do. There is nothing left but for me to return to France!"

Mussolini, eager to appear as the peacemaker, replied, "No! No! Monsieur Daladier! That is not what the Fuehrer meant. . . . He has stressed the fact that apart from the Sudeten districts Germany does not claim any part of Czechoslovak territory. . . ."

When this remark by his Italian confrere was translated, Hitler's tone changed. "Monsieur Daladier," he said pleasantly, "I have expressed myself badly. I do not want any Czechs! Indeed, if you were to offer me the lot, I would not accept a single one!"

Apparently this answer satisfied Chamberlain and Daladier, and the tension lessened. Mussolini took advantage of the more relaxed atmosphere to produce a sheet of paper which he described as being a plan he had drafted to effect a compromise. Actually it was the German demands Von Ribbentrop had given

164

him on the train. Il Duce read the list to the conferees. The major points were:

1. Evacuation of the Sudetenland to begin October 1.

2. Great Britain, France, and Italy to guarantee Germany that the evacuation of territory shall be completed by October 10, without any destruction taking place.

3. An international commission would decide details of evacuation. Its membership to include the four powers and Czechoslovakia.

4. International supervision of the plebiscite and of the final termination of boundaries. An international force to occupy the "disputed" territories.

5. Progressive occupation by the German Army of those zones with a German majority, starting October 1.

Since neither the French Premier nor the British Prime Minister was aware that Mussolini's "plan" had been written by the Germans, they accepted it as a "basis for discussion."

Chamberlain objected, however, that Great Britain could offer no guarantees without the approval of the Czechoslovaks. This was backed by Daladier and brought a minor flareup from Hitler. "If we have to ask the Czechs for their consent to every detail, we shall be here for weeks," he cried. "In the present circumstances, any delay would be terribly dangerous. . . . It's not a German-Czech problem we are dealing with, but a European problem. . . . If Prague can question an agreement signed by our four signatures, it will mean that they are determined to accept nothing but force. . . ."

And Mussolini warned, "Should the Czechs refuse our demands . . . they will have to put up with the military consequences. . . ."

Hitler agreed, however, to let two Czechoslovak representatives "remain in an adjoining room . . . for consultation. . . ."

When the session recessed for lunch at 3:00 P.M., Chamberlain notified the Czechoslovak Embassy of this decision. Prague's ambassador to Berlin, Vojtech Mastny, and Hubert Masarik, a councilor in the Foreign Office, hurried to the Fuehrerhaus where they were locked in an uncomfortable room to await the outcome of the parley. They were never consulted.

When the meeting resumed at 4:30 P.M., Chamberlain seemed to have forgotten the Czechoslovak representatives. He did not mention them again. He was now more concerned with business matters and wanted to know who would compensate the Czechoslovak government for buildings and "other state properties."

This evoked another explosion from Hitler. "The Sudeten Germans paid for them with their taxes. . . . Those buildings have been paid for more than twice over. . . . There will be no indemnity!"

But ex-businessman Chamberlain was not to be put off so easily. He next asked who would pay for the cattle, farm machinery, and household goods which evacuating Czechoslovaks would have to leave behind. Hitler pounded the table with his fist. "We can't waste time over such trifles," he shouted.

Chamberlain quailed under this outburst, and Daladier remained silent. The property of Czechoslovak farmers had been dealt with; there was nothing further to do but draw up Mussolini's proposals into legal terms. Legal consultants attended to the matter while the principals engaged in amiable conversations; they might have been gathered for a social evening rather than to dissect an independent nation.

Daladier was somewhat surprised when Hitler genially remarked, "I who love art . . . and especially architecture, I only know Paris, which is such a beautiful city, by photographs . . . I should like to see your capital and study it and understand it. . . ."

The French Premier's surprise increased when Hermann Goering added, "I have never been to Paris. And I would like very much to go. . . ."

Later, Daladier repeated this to an aide and noted, "Wouldn't we have a fine mess if I invited both of them to Paris? What a reception our people would give that pair!"

By 7:00 P.M., a draft agreement had been worked out, and another adjournment was called until copies could be typed. Hitler invited Daladier, Chamberlain, and their staffs to a banquet

166

at the Fuehrerhaus, but both refused, preferring to return to their hotels.

Neither man was in a mood for a banquet; perhaps they had saved the peace of Europe, but only at a great cost. The Premier returned to the Vier Jahreszeiten, Chamberlain to the Regina. Both brushed aside swarms of eager reporters. Mastny and Masarik were informed by Ashton-Gwatkin that virtual agreement had been reached. "I cannot yet give you details, but you must be prepared for much harsher conditions than those of the Franco-British plan," he said.

"Can we not at least be heard before we are judged?" Masarik pleaded.

"No! Anyone would think you did not realize how difficult the position of France and Britain is! If you only knew how hard it is to deal with Hitler!" Ashton-Gwatkin said. Then he left the unhappy Czechoslovaks, who remained in the "waiting" room to hear the final verdict.

The conference resumed at 10:00 P.M. More rambling talk and the ironing out of petty details continued until nearly 1:00 A.M. At last, the parties agreed to sign. The original of the document was placed on a mahogany table next to an immense and ornate inkpot. Ambassador François-Poncet, who had helped in the final draft, suddenly exclaimed, "What a disgrace! This is how France rewards the only ally who remained faithful to her!" No one paid any attention to his remark.

In a show of cordiality, Mussolini nudged Daladier, saying, "You will be cheered when you get back home!"

The French Premier shook his massive head. "Perhaps. The people will be glad that the peace is saved; but they will not like the price. . . ."

The leaders approached the table in the order they were to sign—Hitler, Chamberlain, Mussolini, and Daladier. Hitler, smiling slightly, dipped the pen into the inkpot, then let out an exclamation of annoyance. The magnificent inkwell was empty. A replacement was hastily made and the signing completed.

Having no further business to transact, the conference broke up after Hitler delivered a rather grumpy farewell talk. Accompanied by Mussolini, and followed by an array of Nazis and Fas-

167

cists in military uniforms, the Fuehrer left the building. The work of the two dictators was completed, but Daladier and Chamberlain still had the unpleasant chore of informing the Czechoslovaks about the final decision.

Chamberlain seemed pleased over the agreement, but Daladier was gloomy. He knew that Czechoslovakia had been effectively dismembered.

Actually, the Munich Agreement fulfilled all of Hitler's Godesberg demands and a bit more; Chamberlain, who had not yielded at Godesberg, gave in at Munich, undoubtedly because the danger of war was more serious than it had been in mid-September.

The pact's terms called for the following: The four governments, having agreed on the cession of the Sudetenland to Germany, now set forth the terms for carrying out the transfer. Czechoslovakia would not be allowed to evade compliance.

By October 1, evacuation would begin; it would be completed on October 10. All installations were to be left intact; the Czechoslovaks were responsible to see that this was accomplished.

An international commission, with members from Germany, Italy, France, Great Britain, and Czechoslovakia would settle the final conditions for the evacuation.

The Czechoslovak government must release all Sudeten Germans from the Armed Forces and the jails. (No provisions were made for the release of Czechoslovaks imprisoned by the Nazis.)

The borders of the new Czechoslovakia would be guaranteed by the four powers—after Hungarian and Polish claims had been settled.

The Munich Pact was no more severe than any peace treaty imposed upon a conquered nation; but in this case, Czechoslovakia had not been defeated in battle, she had been betrayed by allies who chose accommodation over principle.

True, the pact had temporarily prevented a war; but now that Czechoslovakia had been stripped of her fortifications, she lay helpless before Hitler. At any time he chose, the Fuehrer could snuff out the little nation's life.

Daladier and Chamberlain met with Mastny and Masarik at 1:30 A.M. and announced the disastrous news. There was no appeal for the Czechoslovaks. Either accept, they were told, or face

Hitler alone. Weeping, Mastny said with all the dignity he could muster, "We have no choice; we must yield—but all this is not final! It's only a moment in history and will be called to question again. . . ."

Chamberlain's response was a polite yawn; Daladier glowered.

CHAPTER 23

Without consulting either Daladier or his own advisers, Neville Chamberlain added a final touch to his Munich visit. He arranged a meeting with Hitler at 11:00 A.M., September 30, in the Fuehrer's apartment, a modest flat in a middle-class section of Munich.

Chamberlain had come there to talk about a separate Anglo-German friendship pact. In fact, Chamberlain had drawn up a memorandum which he wanted the Fuehrer to read and sign, if he approved it. The document said in part:

We the German Fuehrer and Chancellor and the British Prime Minister . . . are agreed in recognizing that the question of Anglo-German relations is of the first importance for the two countries and for Europe.

We regard the Agreement signed last night . . . as symbolic of the desire of our two peoples never to go to war with one another again.

We are resolved that the method of consultation shall be the method adopted to deal with any other questions that may concern our two countries . . . and we are determined to remove possible sources of difference and thus to contribute to assure the peace of Europe. . . .

Hitler agreed to sign the document, and within moments both men had affixed their signatures. For Chamberlain, this was the supreme moment of his life; he had signed a contract, given his word that war would never again occur between England and

171

tired from politics, to return to his native Vaucluse, an aged man with fading memories.

If there is any moral to be drawn from the 1938 events at Munich, Germany, perhaps it can be summed up in the words of Thomas Jefferson:

"The tree of liberty must be refreshed from time to time with the blood of patriots and tyrants. . . ."

INDEX

175

177

178

France (cont'd)

Georges; Reynaud, Paul); Air Force, 29, 55, 113, 137, 138; alliances and treaties with Czechoslovakia, 51–52, 54, 56, 115, 139, 144 (*see also* Treaties; specific treaties); Army, 28–29, 41, 42, 54, 67, 94, 113, 137, 138, 145, 147, 149; and Benes (*see under* Benes, Eduard); and cession of Sudetenland to Germany, 115–19, 124, 141 ff., 152 ff.; and Chamberlain, 94–96, 110–14, 145, 172; and Czechoslovakia, 33, 34–35, 37, 39–42, 47, 51–52, 54, 56, 62, 63–65, 67–68, 70–71, 77, 82–85, 88, 91–96, 110–14, 115–19, 121, 139, 141 ff., 144, 152 ff.; fears civil war in Czechoslovakia, 91; and Fourth Plan, 88; Franco-Prussian War, 21, 41; and German war preparations, 76; and Godesberg Conference and Memorandum, 136, 142, 144 ff.; and Great Britain, 33, 41, 49, 51–55, 56, 62–65, 67–68, 70–71, 77, 82, 84, 85, 94–96, 110–14, 136–39, 144, 152 ff. (*see also* specific conferences and agreements, individuals); and Hitler (Nazi Germany), 28–29, 41–42, 82–83, 99, 100, 110–14, 173 (*see also* specific conferences and agreements, individuals, issues); and July Crisis, 77; and Karlsbad demands, 49, 82–85, 88; and Maginot Line, 28–29, 54, 67, 94, 136, 138, 145; and May Crisis, 62–65, 67–68, 70–71; and Munich Conference and Agreement, 156, 158, 159, 160–62, 163–69, 172, 173; opposition to war and feeling toward Germans in, 41–42; Popular Front government, 39–42; preparedness for war, 28–29, 136–39, 146, 147–48, 149; and Runciman mission, 77, 82, 84, 85; and Russia, 33,

117, 139; stiffens stand toward Czechoslovakia, 62, 63–65, 67–68, 70–71; urges Czechoslovakia to capitulate to Hitler's demands, 47, 100–14 (*see also* Appeasement); warns Germany France will fight, mobilizes, 93–96; and World War I, 15, 16, 21–23, 25, 28; and World War II, 173

Franco, Francisco, 7, 148; declares his neutrality, 148

François-Poncet, André, 151, 154–55, 156, 167; calls Munich Agreement a disgrace, 167

Franco-Prussian War, 21, 41

Franklin, Benjamin, *quoted*, 13

Franzenbad, 62

Franz Joseph, Emperor, 31

Free Corps (*Frei Korps*), German, 20; in Sudetenland, 59–60, 90, 92–93, 107, 115, 121, 125, 134

Frei Korps. See Free Corps

Fuehrerhaus, Munich, 160, 163, 166, 167

Gamelin, General Maurice G., 54, 94, 137, 138; predicts "grand offensive" in event of war, 94; reports on French preparedness and war tactics, 54, 137, 138–39

Generals' Plot (Generals' Conspiracy), 99–101, 138, 159. *See also* Beck, Ludwig; Holder, Franz

George VI, King of England, 75, 77, 109

German Air Force (Luftwaffe), 28, 55, 64, 76, 83, 135, 137, 138; Hitler and, 28, 100; and Spanish Civil War, 7; strength of, 94, 113

German Army (Wehrmacht), 33–34, 35, 74, 83, 101, 106, 110, 122, 138, 145 (*see also* specific generals, units, wars); and Austrian occupation, 29, 33–34, 35; and Case Green (*see* Case Green); and Czechoslovakia, 33–34, 35,

179

Great Britain (*cont'd*)

Baldwin, Stanley; Benes, Eduard; Chamberlain, Neville; Commons, British House of; Duff-Cooper, Alfred; Halifax, Lord Edward; Henderson, Sir Neville; Hitler, Adolf; MacDonald, Malcolm; Newton, Sir Basil; Simon, Sir John; Wilson, Sir Horace); Air Force (*see* British Air Force); Anglo-German friendship pact (1938), 171–72; and appeasement of Hitler and Nazi Germany (*see* Appeasement; specific individuals, issues); Army (*see* British Army); and cession of Sudetenland to Germany, 49, 51–58, 74–78, 79–85, 88, 90–91, 94–97, 101–7, 109–14, 115–19, 121–26, 141 ff., 151 ff. (*see also* specific conferences and agreements, individuals, issues); change in attitude toward Czechoslovakia in, 62–65; Czechoslovakia urged to appease Nazis, 47 (*see also* Appeasement; specific conferences and agreements; individuals, issues); and Czechoslovak mobilization, 69; Cliveden Set in, 75; fears civil war in Czechoslovakia, 91; and France, 33, 41, 49, 51–55, 56, 62–65, 67–68, 70–71, 77, 82, 84, 85, 94–96, 110–14, 136–39, 144, 152 ff. (*see also* specific conferences and agreements, individuals, issues); and French war preparedness, 136–39; and Godesberg Conference and Memorandum, 121–26, 127–32, 133–36, 137, 141 ff., 151 ff.; Henlein and, 57–58, 81; and Hitler, 28, 39, 68, 74–78, 100 (*see also* specific aspects, individuals, issues); and July Crisis, 74–78; and Karlsbad demands, 49, 51–58, 83–85; and May Crisis, 62–65, 68, 70–71; and Munich Conference and Agreement, 156, 157–62, 163–

69, 171–74 (*see also* Munich Conference and Agreement); Navy (*see* British Navy); rapport with Germany, 75 (*see also* specific individuals); reluctant to fight Hitler, 39, 100; and Runciman mission, 77–78, 79–85, 90–91 (*see also* Runciman, Viscount Walter); war preparedness in, 28, 138, 139, 145, 149; in World War I era, 15, 16, 21–23; and World War II, 173

Groener, Wilhelm, 18, 20, 22

Halder, Franz, 99–100

Halifax, Lord Edward, 38, 39, 51–52, 53, 63–64, 137, 157; and Benes regime, 70, 83; and Chamberlain-Hitler meeting, 101, 113; and May Crisis, 70; and Munich Conference, 158; and Runciman mission, 77, 83; urges Czechoslovaks to capitulate, 56, 83; and Wiedemann message from Hitler on Czechoslovak invasion, 74–75

Hapsburgs, 31

Hearst, William Randolph, 69

Heinkels (German warplanes), 7

Henderson, Ian, 79

Henderson, Sir Neville, 39, 60, 74; calls Hitler "constructive genius," 47; and Chamberlain-Hitler Meetings, 95, 102, 103; and Godesberg Conference and proposals, 122, 128, 129, 141, 144, 145, 151 ff.; and Hitler's Nuremberg address, 92; quoted on apathy to war among German people, 148–49; and Ribbentrop, 62–63; warns Chamberlain on Sudetenland, 76–77, 95

Henlein, Konrad, 32, 34, 45, 47, 59–61; and Benes, 56, 57–58, 73–74; and British, 57–58, 81; flees into Germany, 93; and Fourth Plan, 87, 89; and Free Corps, 115, 134 (*see also* Free Corps: in Sudetenland); and Hitler, 57,

181

Henlein, Konrad (*cont'd*)
73–74, 78; and Karlsbad demands, 48–49, 53, 56, 57–58, 81, 82, 83, 87 (*see also* Karlsbad demands); and Runciman mission, 81, 82, 83, 89
Hess, Rudolf, 75
Hindenburg, Paul von, 15, 18, 19–20, 22; appoints Hitler Chancellor of Germany, 27; death of, 27; heads government, 26
Hitler, Adolf, 29, 32–35, 38, 47, 49, 51–58, 68, 73–78, 82–83, 94–97, 101–7; appeasement policy toward (*see* Appeasement; specific individuals); and Austria, 29, 32, 33, 35; background, comes to power, declares himself Fuehrer, 27; becomes Chancellor, 27; and Beer Hall Putsch, imprisonment of, 26; and Benes, 144, 156; Berlin *Sportspalast* speech, 141–43, 148; and Big Lie technique, 43; Bonnet praises, 82–83; at Breslau, 75–76; and Case Green (*see* Case Green); and Chamberlain (*see* Chamberlain, Neville); and Daladier, 52, 82, 110, 155; described, 43; determined to smash Czechoslovakia, 43, 65, 154; FDR pleas to avoid war to, 139–40, 147; flouts Versailles Treaty, rebuilds Germany, prepares for war, 27–29 (*see also* Versailles Treaty); and Fourth Plan, 88; and France (*see* France; specific conferences and agreements, individuals, issues); and Godesberg Conference and Memorandum, 121–26, 127–32, 139, 141–42 ff.; and Great Britain (*see* Great Britain; specific conferences and agreements, individuals, issues); has second thoughts on war, 146–49 ff.; and Henlein, 57, 73–74, 78; and Hungary, 43–44, 106, 125, 147, 159,

164; and Jews, 24, 25, 26, 27, 28, 43, 92; and last-minute peace attempts, 139–40, 146–49, 151 ff.; letter to Chamberlain, 149; and May Crisis, 64–65, 68; *Mein Kampf*, 26, 43; and Munich Conference and Agreement, 153–56, 157–62, 163–69, 171–73 (*see also* Munich Conference and Agreement); Mussolini and, 147–48, 153–56, 160 (*see also* Mussolini, Benito); Nuremberg address by, 91–93; plans Czechoslovakia invasion, 46–49; and Poland, 44, 106–7, 125, 164, 173; proposes plebiscite, 127; reasons for agreeing to Munich Conference, 159; and Runciman mission, 77–78, 82–83; and Russia, 33, 99; signs Anglo-German friendship pact (1938), 171–72; suicide of, 173; and treaty abrogations, 115; and Versailles Treaty, 23–24, 25, 26, 27, 83, 92; and World War II, 173
Hoare, Sir Samuel, 38
Hodza, Milan, 45, 116; forced to resign, 118; wins vote of confidence, 69
Hoffmann, George, 62
Hohenzollerns, 17 (*see also* specific individuals)
Holy Roman Empire, 27
Hore-Belisha, Leslie, 135, 136
"Horst Wessel Song," 91
Hradschin, Castle, Prague, 114, 115, 116, 118
Hull, Cordell, 68
Hungary, 172; and Czechoslovakia, 31, 32, 33, 35, 43–44, 106, 107, 125, 147, 159, 164, 172; and Czechoslovakia (1968), 8; and Hitler, 43–44, 106, 125, 147, 159, 164; minority in Czechoslovakia, 31, 32, 84, 104, 107, 125, 164
Hurricanes (British aircraft), 28

182

183

184

ABOUT THE AUTHOR

Irving Werstein was born in Brooklyn, New York, and grew up in Richmond Hills, Queens, where he attended Richmond Hill High School. After spending two years at New York University during the height of the Depression, he had to leave in order to look for a job. He became in succession a waiter, an actor, a "borscht circuit" comedian, and a factory worker. Having developed an interest in writing early in life, he continued to write during this period and sold his first story—a Western—in 1938. He has been a free-lance writer ever since.

Mr. Werstein is the author of thirty books for adults and young adults, and his work has appeared in such magazines as *True*, *The Saturday Evening Post*, and *Collier's*. A confirmed traveler, he has lived in England, France, Denmark, Mexico, Italy, and Belgium.

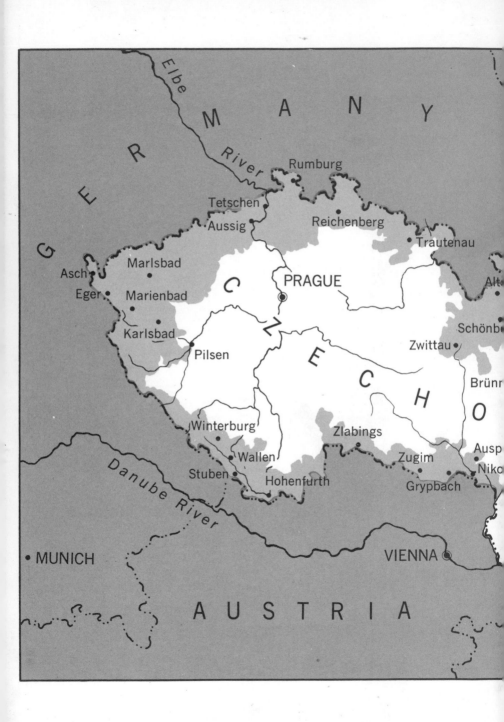